RECLAIMING
THE AMERICAN DREAM

PHILANTHROPY AND SOCIETY
Richard Magat, Series Editor

RECLAIMING THE AMERICAN DREAM

The Role of Private Individuals and Voluntary Associations

Richard C. Cornuelle

With a New Introduction by
Frank Annunziata
and an Afterword by the Author

Transaction Publishers
New Brunswick (U.S.A.) and London (U.K.)

Third printing 2011
New material this edition copyright © 1993 by Transaction Publishers, New Brunswick, New Jersey 08903. Originally published in 1965 by Random House, Inc.

This book is printed on acid-free paper that meets the American National Standard for Permanence of Paper for Printed Library Materials.

Library of Congress Catalog Number: 92-32936
ISBN: 978-1-56000-655-8
Printed in the United States of America

Library of Congress Cataloging-in-Publication Data

Cornuelle, Richard C., 1927-
    Reclaiming the American dream: the role of private individuals and voluntary associations/Richard C. Cornuelle; with an introduction by Frank Annunziata, and an afterword by the author.
        p.   cm. —(Philanthropy and society)
    ISBN 1-56000-655-2 (pbk.)
        1. United States—Social policy. 2. United States—Politics and government—20th century. 3. Right and left (Political science) I. Title. H. Series

HN65.C65   1993
306'.0973—dc20   92-32936
                                                                         CIP

CONTENTS

Introduction to the Transaction Edition   *ix*

A Personal Summary   *xxxi*

1   Resignation, Right and Left   3

BOTH CONSERVATIVES AND LIBERALS FEEL THE TRAGIC FAILURE OF THEIR EQUALLY VALID IDEALS—THE LIMITATION OF GOVERNMENT AND THE PROMPT SOLUTION OF PUBLIC PROBLEMS.

2   Why the Conservatives Can't Win   6

THEY PROTEST WITHOUT A PROGRAM. TO WIN OFFICE, THEY MUST EITHER COMPROMISE THEIR PRINCIPLES OR UNDERBID THEIR LIBERAL COMPETITION.

3   Why the Liberals Can't Win   *13*

THOUGH IN POWER, POURING OUT FEDERAL PILLS FOR ALL ILLS, THEY HAVE LATELY COME TO NOTICE THAT THE MEDICINE IS NOT WORKING.

4   That Was the Dream That Was   20

THE ORIGINAL AMERICAN DREAM OF A SOCIETY THAT WAS BOTH FREE AND HUMANE BECAME A REALITY BECAUSE WE MET MOST PUBLIC NEEDS OUTSIDE GOVERNMENT.

5   The Rediscovery of Independent Action   26

THE KEY TO OUR SYSTEM, LOST IN THE TWENTIETH CENTURY, WAS A THIRD SECTOR, NEITHER COMMERCIAL NOR GOVERNMENTAL, WHICH SOLVED MOST PUBLIC PROBLEMS DIRECTLY.

6   The Independent Sector   35

THE TREMENDOUS RAW POWER AND RESOURCES OF THE CENTRAL SECTOR OF AMERICAN SOCIETY ARE LARGELY IGNORED, AND ITS ACCOMPLISHMENTS TAKEN FOR GRANTED.

7 *The Failure of the Independent Sector* 42

BECAUSE IT HAS NOT ADOPTED MODERN TECHNOLOGY, AS INDUSTRY AND GOVERNMENT HAVE, THE INDEPENDENT SECTOR SEEMS BACKWARD AND UNRELIABLE.

8 *What Took Us So Long?* 47

AS COMMERCE BLOSSOMED WHEN ITS MOVING FORCES WERE UNDERSTOOD AND LEGITIMATIZED, SO THE INDEPENDENT SECTOR CAN EXPAND IF ITS FUNCTION IS CLEARLY UNDERSTOOD AND ITS MACHINERY MODERNIZED.

9 *The Independent Sector's Driving Force* 55

THE IMPULSE TO SERVE IS AN OVERRIDING HUMAN INSTINCT COMPARABLE TO THE DESIRE FOR PROFIT OR POWER.

10 *The Independent Sector's Discipline* 65

DIRECT COMPETITION WITH GOVERNMENT FOR PUBLIC SERVICE, NOW CONSIDERED ILLEGITIMATE (AS THE PURSUIT OF PROFIT ONCE WAS), CAN BRING THE INDEPENDENT SECTOR TO ITS FULL POTENTIAL.

11 *Accepting the Competitive Challenge* 80

IN A SOCIAL EXPERIMENT WE SET UP AN INDEPENDENT COMPETITOR TO THE FEDERAL STUDENT-LOAN PROGRAM, AND SERVED STUDENTS BETTER.

12 *How to Compete with Government* 90

INDEPENDENT ORGANIZATIONS MUST ADOPT THE PRACTICAL TACTICS OF A BUSINESS CAMPAIGN—FROM RESEARCH TO THE HARD-SELL.

13 *Business and the Public Business* 107

AS THE NATURAL LEADERS OF THE INDEPENDENT SECTOR, BUSINESSMEN UNDERSTAND THE NEED FOR INDEPENDENT PUBLIC SERVICE BUT ARE JUST LEARNING HOW TO MAKE IT WORK.

14   *The Giant Stirs*   125

ALMOST UNCONSCIOUSLY, MANY PEOPLE ARE SUDDENLY
BEGINNING TO ADAPT THE INDEPENDENT IMPULSE TO
TWENTIETH-CENTURY CONDITIONS.

15   *The Churches: Center of Concern*   135

IF CHURCHES RECLAIM THEIR SERVICE MISSION, TEM-
PORARILY GIVEN OVER TO GOVERNMENT, THEY CAN
TRANSFORM THE WHOLE SOCIETY.

16   *Foundations: Citizen Risk Capital*   143

FOUNDATIONS NOW TEST-RUN PROGRAMS FOR GOVERN-
MENT, BUT TO SURVIVE THEY MUST COMPETE WITH IT.

17   *Chief Citizens in Politics*   153

MORE AND MORE FEDERAL AND STATE EXECUTIVES ARE
SEARCHING FOR WAYS TO ENCOURAGE INDEPENDENT
ACTION, BUT HAVE FOUND THEY CAN'T GIVE RESPON-
SIBILITY TO PEOPLE WHO DO NOT FIRST DEMAND IT.

18   *Big Brotherhood or a Free Society*   166

TECHNOLOGY CAN BE AN ENSLAVING FORCE IF GOVERN-
MENT MONOPOLIZES IT. BUT IF THE INDEPENDENT SEC-
TOR LEARNS TO USE IT, TECHNOLOGY CAN BE A GREAT
EMANCIPATING FORCE.

Afterword   170

Introduction to the
Transaction Edition

Richard Cornuelle's *Reclaiming the American Dream* is now thirty years old; it belongs to the category of works deserving republication a generation after making its first appearance. It is fresh, lucid, engaging, and memorable. This was the book where the term "independent sector" originated and gained popularity. Sometimes too discursive, often too understated and underdeveloped, still it succeeded in being read by the diverse audiences comprising the voluntary sector. It also attracted a broad intellectual response. Refreshingly free from cant and rancor, the book's voice was authentic, appealing, and inclusive—the voice of the tradition of limited government, yet one with a human face. In its best moments, the book is singularly free from what Albert Hirschman has called the "rhetoric of reaction." This is the rhetorical style that invokes rationales against social reform by citing why "perversity, futility and jeopardy" will always emerge as factors despoiling meliorist efforts.[1] In its weaker moments, as when it groped for a historical story line to buttress and sustain whatever claims were being made for the development of voluntarism, it claimed greater attention from ideological and political sources than from the foundation establishment or scholars of philanthropy.

The author deserves to savor its reputation as a classic. Not only did Cornuelle craft the book's major themes artfully, but he deftly and gently interpolated autobiographical episodes that illumined his own work as a foundation executive. Particularly notable are his outstanding achievements in establishing the United Student Aid Funds and the Foundation for Voluntary Welfare, which later became the Center for Independent Action. They stand as impressive and instructive exemplars of voluntary service.

Robert Bremner's *American Philanthropy*, a book that Richard Magat has described as a "modest masterpiece which lives in every bibliography of voluntarism and philanthropy" and "is the starting point for both casual readers and academic scholars," recognized that Cornuelle's *Reclaiming the American Dream* represented an important facet of anti-statist thought and placed it on his list of important dates in the history of American philanthropy. Bremner rendered its thesis as advocating "reliance on voluntary organizations rather than 'unlimited government' as [the] best solution to social problems."[2]

In the memoir he has prepared for this edition Cornuelle discusses his intellectual relationship with Professor Ludwig von Mises at New York University in the years after World War II. He also explains why he found the critique of socialism and welfare state liberalism that Friedrich von Hayek was concurrently developing so persuasive. *Reclaiming the American Dream* derived many of its insights from this libertarian intellectual tradition, especially from Hayek's *The Road to Serfdom* (1944).

Hayek attributed to Alexis de Tocqueville the "acute insight" to "foresee the psychological effects of the modern welfare state." So provocative was Tocqueville's insight into a "new kind of servitude," said Hayek, that it had, in fact, inspired the title of his own new book *The Road to Serfdom*. Hayek believed that this passage from Tocqueville captured the essence of Europe and the United States at the end of World War II:

> After having thus successively taken each member of the community in its powerful grasp, and fashioned him at will, the supreme power then extends its arm over the whole community. It covers the surface of society with a network of small complicated rules, minute and uniform, through which the most original minds and the most energetic characters cannot penetrate to rise above the crowd. The will of man is not shattered but softened, bent and guided; men are seldom forced by it to act, but they are constantly restrained from acting. Such a power does not destroy, but it prevents existence; it does not tyrannize, but it compresses, enervates, extinguishes, and stupefies a people, till each nation is reduced to being nothing better than a flock of timid and industrial animals, of which government is the shepherd—I have always thought that servitude of the regular, quiet, and gentled kind which I have just described might be combined more easily than is commonly believed with some of the outward forms of freedom and that it might even establish itself under the wing of the sovereignty of the people.[3]

This Tocqueville/Hayek refrain suffuses Cornuelle's book, especially in his definition of the foundation:

> The foundation is an instrument forged by citizens who transfer profit from the commercial sector and put it directly to work as risk capital for the general betterment of the society. To say or imply that the foundation exists only on the sufferance of government is to reason from the premise that government is the whole society. Here is a special version of the untenable notion that the citizen and all his institutions are creatures of the state, not the other way around. The government has no natural "burden," no

divine franchise on public responsibility. It simply does the chores we have for it to do.[4]

Thirty years ago, in 1962, as Clinton Rossiter was revising the best study we have of the conservative tradition in American history *Conservatism in America*, he reflected upon its prospects. In his judgment, conservatism needed to move beyond sterile and strident anti-statism. Although Rossiter believed that the "confusions of American conservative thought have had a depressing influence on the art of public debate, the advance of social justice, the solution of persistent problems of a complex industrial society, and the identification and defense of the primary values in our tradition,"[5] he also understood that however beset with difficulties conservatism was, its skillful "sponsorship and leadership of voluntary associations" was its indisputable and indispensable achievement. Thus, "the association for charitable, cultural, economic, or social purposes is America's characteristic institution. It ensures progress because it pools the hopes and talents of free individuals and breeds natural leaders; it brings stability because it balances the American ideal of self-reliance against the universal urge for communal association; it defends liberty because it serves as buffer between man and government, doing things for him that he cannot do for himself and must not let government do for him."[6] This facet of conservatism rarely appeared in conservative commentary. With Cornuelle's *Reclaiming the American Dream*, it would receive a noteworthy restatement.

The prototypical conservative argument was a litany of imprecation structured in a grammar of denunciation deploring "welfarist-socialist-inflationist trends" and envisioning "not more paternalism, laws, decrees and controls, but the restoration of liberty and free enterprise, the restoration of incentives to let loose the tremendous constructive energies of 200 million Americans."[7] *Reclaiming the American Dream* was so different in tone and substance from the normative conservative expression that it met with varied responses. For reasons that Cornuelle explains in the afterword to this volume, when in December 1964 *Look* magazine published its own description of his work in an article entitled "The New Conservative Manifesto," a political emphasis rather than one on the evolution and significance of America's non-governmental institutions came to prevail as the defining characterization of *Reclaiming the American Dream.*

> Random House promptly bought *Reclaiming the American Dream* and I began to receive altogether unprecedented numbers of letters, calls and propositions of various kinds, many of them from politicians. In this way, a movement that was not conservative came to be called conservative, and a non-political, even antipolitical approach to public policy, came to be seen as a new and promising political strategy. My judgment having been clouded by the unfamiliar attention, I agreed to these misrepresentations, an error I have since come to regret most deeply. The untruth in labeling was of course much less important than the unnatural politicalization of a position that will not succeed until it is understood, not just as non-political, but as counter-political. This became the principal defect of the movement and the book. [8]

The tension inherent in deriving political solutions from Cornuelle's work can be seen in *National Review* editor Frank Meyer's argument with T George Harris of *Look* magazine that Cornuelle's proposals could not thrive in "an atmosphere dominated by Liberal statism." "They depend for their visibility," Meyer asserted, "on a society of free economy and limited government. They do not rival, rather they complement conservative political action. They add a necessary dimension to the conservative endeavor."[9]

In fact, it was Frank Meyer—one of the most intellectually gifted and rigorously honest and searching conservative intellectuals—who called upon *National Review* readers to confront Cornuelle's challenge. Like Whittaker Chambers, who had predicted that a conservatism bereft of positive initiatives in the face of social disorder would be a conservatism of "futility and petulance," Meyer insisted that "conservatives are not [S]ocial Darwinians." Whatever Meyer's enthusiasm was for Cornuelle's appealing rationale, and it was considerable, he pierced to the essence of the independent, voluntarist predicament by lamenting the impediments to fulfilling Cornuelle's vision. Meyer believed it was "the increasing impersonalization of modern society [that made] the personal relationship between those who need help and those who want to help them very hard to achieve."[10]

Meyer's recognition of this dilemma in 1965 might be contrasted with Charles Murray's preface to Marvin Olasky's 1992 study *The Tragedy of American Compassion.* Murray submits that the book's "central truth" is its exposition of how "human needs were answered by other human beings, not by bureaucrats, and the response to those needs was not compartmentalized." Here Murray asserts that "the modern welfare state must be dismantled,"[11] but offers no commensurate insights into how to reorient citizens away from the governmental habit that Cornuelle and Meyer hoped to stimulate. Consider, specifically, Cornuelle's praise for the voluntary sector's work with the poor:

> Those who are succeeding with the poor, helping them climb out of poverty—like the Y.M.C.A., Urban League, community welfare councils—are indepen-

dent institutions. It seems logical then to subsidize the independent institutions. And, just as logically, that is how to kill them. You can almost see the work slow down and the "coordination" begin, the substitution of administrators for workers. And then the paper blizzard. The tragedy is that the final effect of the poverty program may be to destroy the agencies which could eliminate poverty. [12]

At the end of Chapter 6 in *Reclaiming the American Dream*, a moral earnestness and passion inspire the exuberant and expansive program that he believes the independent sector can accomplish. No comparable vision exists by Murray or Olasky.

This was the case in the mid-sixties as well for American conservatives. In 1967, Frank Meyer, for example, once again appealed to his colleagues on the Right about the particular virtues in Cornuelle's approach:

> But to maintain that hardships, deprivations, social imbalances are not properly or effectively solved by government action is not to deny their existence. Rather it is to call upon the imaginative exercise of voluntary altruistic efforts to invigorate a widespread sense of responsibility for social well-being and to guard against the moral degradation of direct clients of the state or as indirect petitioners for community largesse. Some idea of what could be done in this way has been projected by Richard C. Cornuelle both descriptively in his book *Reclaiming the American Dream*, and practically in the work of the Fund for Voluntary Welfare. [13]

When Harvard University Press reprinted, in 1982, Rossiter's *Conservatism in America*, it was accompanied by a foreword by George Will. Nothing appeared to have changed among conservatives from 1962 to 1982, because Will reproached his colleagues on the

Right for their signal failure—for failing to acknowledge how the

> severely individualistic values, and the atomizing social dynamism of a capitalistic society conflict with the traditional and principled conservative concern with . . . the life of society in its gentling corporate existence—in communities, churches, and other institutions that derive their usefulness and dignity from their ability to summon individuals up from individualism to concerns larger and longer-lasting than their self-interestedness. [14]

But Will's plea for community was, as we have already seen, a luminous theme throughout *Reclaiming the American Dream*, and Cornuelle would make it again in *Healing America* (1983):

> In the end, a good society is not so much the result of grand designs and bold decisions, but of millions upon millions of small caring acts, repeated day after day, until direct mutual action becomes second nature and to see a problem is to begin to wonder how to best act on it.
>   And, if someday America succeeds in reviving its sense of community, we will surely wonder in retrospect how we ever thought we could sustain a good society without individual effort. [15]

It is a testament to Rossiter's powers of insight and generalization to recall that no excerpts from *Reclaiming the American Dream*, nor from any of Cornuelle's two other books or essays, nor from any kindred sources, were ever included in William F. Buckley's anthologies of conservative writing. George Nash's 1976 study, *The Conservative Intellectual Movement in America Since 1945*, did, however, take notice of Richard Cornuelle as "one unorthodox conservative" whose "brisk little book won quick acclaim in conservative circles and from such unexpected sources as Saul Alinsky."[16]

Given that Cornuelle made only peripheral references to the historical complexities pertaining to the development of voluntary activities and philanthropic enterprises, it is not surprising that exhortation substituted for analysis at critical junctures. While there were many celebratory anecdotes about voluntarism in the American past, corresponding careful consideration of the relevant historical circumstances and conditions was absent from the book. To readers who thought his historical interpretation was "simplistic," Cornuelle readily conceded that "this is not the book, nor am I the historian, to provide the elaborate documentation of the detailed evolution of our non-governmental institutions. My purpose is to start rather than finish a search for better understanding of this tradition."[17]

One significant exposition of the voluntary tradition inheres in Daniel Boorstin's interpretation of American ideas and institutions. Boorstin gives primacy to the historical importance of our communities being voluntary, of our communities preceding governments, of designing "purposes" before "machinery," unlike Europe, where "the charitable spirit was a kind of residuum" and "inevitably tended to become the spirit of almsgiving." Boorstin contraposed the influential example of Benjamin Franklin, who cared not whether "the job was done by government or by individuals: both . . . were agencies of community. The community was the thing."[18]

Robert Bremner, the leading historian of American philanthropy, has explained why philanthropy has been "one of the principal methods of social advance" and that "voluntary benevolence has played a large role and performed important functions in American society." Bremner's scholarship indicates, however, that it is untenable to posit "a basic hostility between public and private activities in the field of welfare in American history" because these relations, while "not always harmonious, have been cooperative and complementary rather than antagonistic."[19]

> Private philanthropists (including voluntary associations) assisted public authorities by assuming responsibility for certain categories or classes of the needy (e.g., aged widows of Methodist ministers or children of Irish Catholic seafarers); public authorities recognized the usefulness of services performed by private charitable organizations by granting them tax exemptions and subsidies from public funds; and in cases involving wills, American courts generally adopted a permissive rather than restrictive attitude toward bequests for "pious and charitable uses." Traditionally Americans assumed that assistance offered by private charity was of a better quality and less demeaning in its consequences than public; even the most ardent supporters of voluntary efforts ordinarily recognized however, that public agencies must bear the heavy burden of caring for unfortunates without family, relatives or friends.[20]

Other features of nineteenth-century philanthropy as well suggested how complex and tangled the historical web of voluntarism was. Andrew Carnegie's philanthropic preferences embraced only those who were "industrious and ambitious," those "most anxious and able to help themselves." Let the state seek out "the irreclaimably destitute, shiftless, and worthless," "the inert, lazy and hopelessly—poor." Bremner concluded that "this division of labor was as much a matter of necessity as of choice. Experience during and after the Civil War had repeatedly demonstrated that philanthropy lacked the resources to assist more than a fraction of those in need, whether soldiers, freedmen, or victims of disaster or depression. Pejorative language aside, and even if reluctant to assume the burden, the *state* had to bear major responsibility for social welfare."[21]

Many of the intellectual and political developments of the last three decades have perhaps endowed Cornuelle's book with an unforeseen relevance to changing conditions. Rather than representing the final spasm of a dispirited, declinist tradition, *Reclaiming the American Dream* endures as a lucid, compelling invocation of the voluntary spirit in American history. Published in the midst of an absence of intellectual curiosity about the independent sector and widespread indifference even among scholars, the work helped to shape a new intellectual climate of awareness and receptivity to the voluntary, independent sector's significance.

Oscar Handlin explained in 1958 that "the weakness of the New Deal, which became apparent only in retrospect, had been to enshrine security as the preeminent social value; liberty was a term all but abandoned to the reactionaries. If the needs of the decade dictated that emphasis, it nevertheless left the masses of people uneducated to the importance of issues wider than their own material safety and well being."[22] He was expressing a minority view, one clearly relegated to marginal status intellectually and politically. But ten years later a neoconservative perspective had appeared in the work of some academic social scientists. Daniel Moynihan would write about "Where Liberals Went Wrong," and the ideological and generational tensions marking the strife of America in the 1960s could be seen in a historian of Progressivism, Louis Filler, decrying the appropriation of the term compassion "by liberal advocates of government social programs for the poor and needy. The implication has been that only those who advocate such programs can be said to have compassion."[23] Cornuelle wants us to remember that while a "tentative renaissance" has marked the independent sector since the mid-1960s, we should not forget that "for half a century, the third sector was in limbo, the victim of an unexamined supposition that in an industrial society, organized social action outside the state was technologically obsolete."[24]

This contention of Cornuelle's has received renewed attention in recent scholarship. James Davison Hunter, a sociologist at the University of Virginia, has expressed similar reservations about the politicization of society:

> Not only has the government assumed more and more jurisdiction over areas of social life previously controlled by the churches and synagogues but it has also been less and less inclined to assist religious organizations as they attempt to contribute to the public good, through, for example, religiously based education and welfare services. Second, a secular orientation is manifested in the way the modern state is organized from its highest to lowest echelons according to bureaucratic principles. Thus the *very ethos* of the modern state is unsupportive of a broad cultural system rooted and legitimated by, and promoting (through public policy) a commitment to transcendent ideals.[25]

Hunter worries, as did Cornuelle earlier, about the geographic locations of the centers of cultural activism. Since cities were "the political nucleus of national life and the region from which the larger cultural warfare emanates," Hunter appreciates how much more difficult it is for the conservative voluntarist perspective "to alter the ethos of national public life for those operating in large measure from the periphery of social power than for those whose efforts are concentrated in the center."[26]

A few years before Hunter's study, George Weigel, a Catholic intellectual, had also warned why "religiously-based philanthropies need not accept the American secular left's approach to American moral culture or contemporary American social problems:"

> A religiously-grounded approach to philanthropy will stress the ways in which social problems must be addressed at their roots—which are usually cultural, not "structural," and which may well involve moral education and character-formation of the kind that governmentally-funded squadrons of social workers are singularly unable (or unwilling) to provide. Here is an important point at which the most recent academic research on the future of social welfare policy and the instincts of religiously-based donors coincide. [27]

Especially over the course of the last decade, the growth and intensity of interest in the role of private philanthropy and voluntarism in American life has been remarkable. Research on philanthropic foundations, charitable trusts, and the nonprofit sector generally is underway, and so too are efforts to reassess the role of public philanthropy. Republication of this volume will, therefore, be useful to many. But since philanthropy's dominant tradition, and its prevailing wisdom, stresses that voluntary action supplement and complement but never supplant government responsibility for citizens' well-being, Richard Cornuelle has marginal rather than mainstream status in the field.

As he makes clear in his afterword, Cornuelle deems this "complementary" stance "short-sighted, self-defeating, and almost totally mistaken. The sector must see itself not as an instrument of the state but as an essential alternative to the state."[28] In contending that "most of the agencies in the philanthropic subsector of the independent sector have become quasi-governmental" by misunderstanding "their mission and their right relation to the state,"[29] Cornuelle is posing

anew a whole ensemble of questions that need to be
met not with reflexive, ritualistic responses, nor with
indifference. So, those responsible for selecting this
volume for republication have demonstrated an ad-
mirable commitment to the competition of ideas and to
a vital aspect of diversity, albeit one that is today
rarely nurtured—the diversity of social thought.

Near the end of the Reagan decade, Alan Pifer, former president of the Carnegie Corporation, surveyed
the voluntary sector and summarized "the principal
characteristics of the current environment for
philanthropy: an apparent decline of compassion for
the unfortunate and neglect of the needs of children;
dissolution of the public/private partnership as a
mechanism for attacking social ills as a result of
federal budget cuts; a turning to the needs of middle-
class clients and to profit-making activities by
voluntary agencies, to ensure their survival; the development of a faddish interest in privatization of human services, with what consequences we know not;
and considerable uncertainty about the future of the
welfare state."[30] This is manifestly not what Cornuelle's assessment resembles. He does not describe
the contemporary voluntary sector in Pifer's terms; he
still asks contemporary establishment leaders of the
independent sector to arouse themselves from torpor
and passivity. "To compete with government and win,"
Cornuelle contends, "you have to perform. But that's
not enough; you also have to let the public know you're
performing. Government is the master huckster of its
plans and programs. The independent sector—humble
and reticent, mute and invisible—has been no good at
all. The public forgets it exists."[31] And still reflecting
the sources of his Hayek/Mises anti-statist critique, he
dissents from the reigning paradigm: "Independent
sector leaders genially speak of complementing government, not competing with it—as if monopoly were

good and competition destructive—thus unwittingly conspiring against the public interest. Without having to match the effort of one outfit against another, neither an independent nor a governmental institution can operate efficiently. Like government, independent institutions are ineffective largely because they no longer compete."[32]

His quarrel with president Reagan, who intoned at the outset of his Presidency that "with the same energy that Franklin Roosevelt sought government solutions" to problems, we will seek private solutions, will not surprise any readers of *Reclaiming the American Dream*:

> The so-called Reagan revolution was bogus—a disguised tax revolt. It was not an effort to repeal the service state but to preserve it—and to substitute debt or inflation for taxation as a way of paying its politically irreducible costs. But the illusion that gave the Reagan programme its ephemeral plausibility has already faded, and America's social democracy is caught in a contradiction from which there is no convenient exit. The status quo is impossible to defend and impossible to change. The American policy is reaching a dead end, and libertarian thought, in its present state of development, doesn't help. [33]

Cornuelle's own social thought, however, has helped, and it is likely to be instrumental in creating the awareness that Peter Drucker believes necessary for America's future. "Government has become too big, too complex, too remote for each citizen actively to participate in it," according to Drucker. "Yet we no longer believe, as did the 'liberals' and 'progressives' these past hundred years, that community tasks can—nay, should—be left to government. As a volunteer the individual can again find active, effective citizenship, can again make a difference, can again exercise control.

This is a uniquely American achievement; it may well be America's most important contribution today." [34]

Frank Annunziata

Notes

1. Albert O. Hirschman, *The Rhetoric of Reaction: Perversity, Futility, Jeopardy* (Cambridge, MA: Belknap Press of Harvard University Press, 1991), 7. An earlier abbreviated version of Hirschman's thesis appeared in "Reactionary Rhetoric," *The Atlantic Monthly*, May 1989.
2. Robert H. Bremner, *American Philanthropy* (Chicago: University of Chicago Press, 1988), 230; Richard Magat, "A Classic Revisited II: Mr. Bremner's Modest Masterpiece," *Foundation News* (July/August 1985), 54-55, 57.
3. Friedrich von Hayek, *The Road to Serfdom* (Chicago: University of Chicago Press, 1944), p. xvi. Hayek's differentiation between true liberals and conservatives is on page xii. Cornuelle's self-description as a libertarian follows this usage. My use of conservative follows the conventional American scholarly and journalistic form wherein libertarian is encompassed within the various forms of conservative thought.
4. Richard Cornuelle, *Reclaiming the American Dream* (New York: Random House, 1965), 151-52.
5. Clinton Rossiter, *Conservatism in America* (Cambridge, MA: Harvard University Press, 1982), 216.
6. Ibid., 253.
7. Henry Hazlitt, *Man vs. the Welfare State* (New Rochelle, NY: Arlington House, 1969), 215.
8. Richard Cornuelle in afterword, this edition.

9. Frank S. Meyer, *The Conservative Mainstream* (New Rochelle, NY: Arlington House, 1969), 202-3.

10. Ibid.

11. See Charles Murray's preface to Marvin Olasky's *The Tragedy of American Compassion* (Washington, DC: Regnery Gateway, 1992), xv-xvi. Gertrude Himmelfarb maintains that despite our triumphs of industrial and social progress "it is poverty that still strikes the eye and strikes at the heart." She speculates that perhaps our "modern sensibility can only register failure, not success, as if modernity has bequeathed to us a social conscience that is unappeasable and inconsolable," and concludes that our "new moral imagination" can no longer take comfort in the ancient adage, "for ye have the poor always with you." Himmelfarb, *The Idea of Poverty: England in the Early Industrial Age* (New York: Random House, 1983), 533-34.

12. Cornuelle, *Reclaiming*, 161.

13. Meyer, *Conservative Mainstream*, 283-84. It is important to distinguish Conuelle's Center for Independent Action from the organization Independent Sector, which came into being in 1980 as a coalition (with more than seven hundred members now) of corporate, foundation and voluntary organization members with national interest and impact in philanthropy and voluntary action. Independent Sector has lobbied in Congress and in federal agencies in the interest of the nonprofit sector and has nurtured research on giving and volunteering.

14. George Will, foreword to Rossiter's, *Conservatism*, ix.

15. Richard Cornuelle, *Healing America* (New York: G. P. Putnam's Sons, 1983), 196. The distance between Cornuelle's sense of the voluntary community and the way present-day leaders of the Republican Party think about its use can be seen in Newt Gingrich's *Window of Opportunity: A Blueprint for the Future* (New York: Tor Books/St. Martin's Press, 1984), where it appears as the seventh point in his program for an "opportunity society," 266.

16.   George H. Nash, *The Conservative Intellectual Movement In America: Since 1945* (New York: Basic Books, 1976), 283-84. Louis Filler in his *Dictionary of American Conservatism* (New York: Philosophical Library, 1987) includes a reference to Cornuelle's *De-Managing America: The Final Revolution* (New York: Random House, 1975) as "an influential book among conservatives," but has no reference to *Reclaiming the American Dream*. See the entry on "Volunteer Action" on 353-54 and 95. On conservative social thought, see William F. Buckley, *Did You Ever See A Dream Walking? American Conservative Thought in the Twentieth Century* (Indianapolis, IN: Bobbs-Merrill Co., 1970) and the revised edition entitled *Keeping The Tablets: Modern American Thought* (New York: Harper and Row, 1988). See also, Jeffrey Hart, *The American Dissent: A Decade of Modern Conservatism* (New York: Doubleday Co., 1966). For an earlier compilation that includes the New Deal Era, see A. G. Heinsohn Jr., *Anthology of Conservative Writing in the United States: 1932-1960* (Chicago: Henry Regnery Co., 1962).

17.   Cornuelle, *Reclaiming*, 22-23. One of the very few single volume histories of the United States that takes note of our voluntary tradition is Rowland Berthoff's *An Unsettled People: Social Order and Disorder in American History* (New York: Harper and Row, 1971). See specially chapter 17 at 451-54 and 471-79.

18.   Daniel Boorstin's superb essay "From Charity to Philanthropy" is included in an imaginatively conceived and thoughtfully edited anthology—Brian O'Connell, *America's Voluntary Spirit* (New York: The Foundation Center, 1983), 129-41. Richard Cornuelle's *Reclaiming* is excerpted on 277-85. For an example of the scholarship he was asking for in 1965, see Anne Firor Scott's major new study of how women's voluntary associations shaped American social history—*Natural Allies: Women's Associations in American History* (Urbana: University of Illinois Press, 1992). "This literature has yet to be written," said Cornuelle in 1965, "but, in time," he believed,

"it could become as rich and extensive as the literature of political economy." Cornuelle, *Reclaiming*, 146.

19. Robert H. Bremner, *The Public Good: Philanthropy and Welfare in the Civil War Era* (New York: Alfred A. Knopf, 1980), xvi.

20. Ibid. For a valuable set of reflections on philanthropists and social control, see Bremner's distinctions on xviii.

21. Ibid., 222.

22. Oscar Handlin, *Al Smith and His America* (Boston: Little Brown and Co., 1958), 187.

23. Daniel P. Moynihan, "Where Liberals Went Wrong," in Melvin R. Laird, ed., *Republican Papers* (New York: Doubleday Anchor Books, 1968), 129-42; Filler, *Dictionary of Conservatism*, 79-80. See also, Frank Annunziata, "The New Left and the Welfare State: The Rejection of American Liberalism," *The Southern Quarterly*, vol. XV (October, 1976), 33-56. On this aspect of Left/Right convergence, see the incident related in Michael Harrington's autobiography *The Long-Distance Runner: An Autobiography* (New York: Henry Holt and Co., 1988), 247.

24. Richard Cornuelle, "New Work for Invisible Hands," *Times Literary Supplement*, 5 April 1991, 1 and ff. For the way Cornuelle anticipated contemporary criticism on the complacent, collaborative aspects of the foundation/government partnership, see Irving Kristol's 1980 address before the Annual Conference of the Council of Foundations, "Foundations and the Sin of Pride: The Myth of the 'Third Sector'" (New York: Institute for Educational Affairs, 1980). This is an important statement which unfortunately did not appear either as one of the selections in Brian O'Connell's anthology on *America's Voluntary Spirit* (New York: The Foundation Center, 1983) or among the nearly six hundred bibliographical citations in its appendix. Daniel Boorstin made a similar judgement when he contended that "generally speaking, instead of being an incentive to the initiative of individuals or communities, our largest foundations have tended to foster (as, indeed, they

Reclaiming the American Dream

created) the vogue for concocted projects cast in the foundation mold. Their proper role," said Boorstin, "is as catalyst." Boorstin, loc. cit., 140.

25. James Davison Hunter, *Culture Wars: The Struggle to Define America* (New York: Basic Books, 1991), 301-02. Richard Lyman's speech at the Fall, 1980 meeting of Independent Sector "What Kind of Society Shall We Have?" had praise for Edmund Burke's passion for the "little platoons." This is reprinted in O'Connell's, *America's Voluntary Spirit*, 371-76.

26. Hunter, *Culture Wars*, 302-3.

27. George Weigel, "Religious Philanthropy's Distinctive Mission," *Philanthropy* (July-August, 1988), 1, 5, 7.

28. Cornuelle, see afterword, this edition.

29. Ibid. Lord Beveridge offered the following distinction about this as early as 1948: "Voluntary Action cannot depend wholly or mainly on help from the State and need not do so." It was "needed to do the things which the State should not do or was most unlikely to do and to pioneer ahead of the State and make experiments." He went on to advise future use of "the term 'Social Service' to mean something done by the State or under its authority, as Social Insurance was used in my first Report to mean insurance organized by the State. The theme of this Report is that the State cannot see to the rendering of all the services that are needed to make a good society. One way of making this point would be to describe simply as Voluntary Services what is done by individual citizens, to supplement what is done as Social Service by the State." Lord Beveridge, *Voluntary Action, A Report on Methods of Social Advance* (New York: The Macmillan Company, 1948), 301-4. See also, R. H. S. Crossman, *The Role of the Volunteer in Modern Social Service* (Oxford: Oxford University Press, 1973) and his *The Gift of Blood* which was excerpted in *Trans-Action*, vol. 8 (January 1971), 18-26, 61-66 and Ralph Kramer, *Voluntary Agencies in the Welfare State* (1981).

30. Alan Pifer, "Philanthropy, Voluntarism and Changing Times," *Daedalus* (Winter, 1987), 126. For data on patterns of giving by Americans from 1955

through 1985, see Bremner, *American Philanthropy*, 178-79 and Brian O'Connell, "Already 1,000 Points of Light," *New York Times*, 25 January 1989. For other perspectives on the Reagan years, see Stuart Butler, *Voluntarism and the Reagan Economic Program* (Washington, DC: Heritage Foundation, November 1981); Alan Pifer, "Philanthropy, Voluntarism and Changing Times," *Daedalus* (Winter 1987), 125; Robert Wuthnow, *Acts of Compassion: Caring for Others and Helping Ourselves* (Princeton: Princeton University Press, 1991); Lindley H. Clark Jr., "Reagan's Safety Net has a Few Holes," *Wall Street Journal*, 20 December 1983, 31; James Keller, "Alms Buildup: Why the Reagan Years are Good for Charity," *Policy Review* (Winter, 1986), 77-78. For a broader analysis of the Reagan presidency and one that is sharply critical from a conservative intellectual, see Robert Nisbet, *The Present Age: Progress and Anarchy in Modern America* (New York: Harper and Row, 1988), 60-62.

31.   Cornuelle, *Reclaiming*, 104.
32.   Ibid., 79.
33.   Cornuelle, "New Work for Invisible Hands," *Times Literary Supplement*, 5 April 1991.
34.   Peter Drucker, "The Non-Profits Quiet Revolution," *Wall Street Journal*, 8 September 1988. Many themes which Cornuelle used in his 1965 book were essentially aspects of one phenomenon viz., "politicization." Two years after *Reclaiming* was published the American edition of Jacques Ellul's *The Political Illusion* was published by Alfred A. Knopf. Since it is the best delineation of the contemporary process wherein the political imperative dominates, it extends the argument of Tocqueville and Hayek.

A PERSONAL SUMMARY

My father was a Presbyterian minister, so I grew up in a series of chilly Presbyterian manses in forgotten little towns in Indiana. Father died in 1938, when I was ten. He left Mother a life insurance policy, a Presbyterian pension, and three boys to raise. He left deep in me the notion that I had been put in the world for some purpose, and that the main business of my life was to find that purpose and do something about it.

For a while, it seemed easy. I had heard no "call" to preach, so I decided instead to devote my life to helping sick people get better. I took a pre-medical course at Occidental College in Southern California, but I didn't intend to practice medicine in the usual way. I wanted to qualify as an M.D. and then spend my life promoting the socialization of medicine. I was not moved by an abstract belief in socialism: I scarcely knew what socialism was. My motive was much simpler. There were obviously a lot of people who needed more and better medical care. Socialized medicine seemed to be the natural way to help them.

Then, in the midst of my studies, polio laid me low. The doctors sent me to bed for nearly a year. For lack of anything else to do, I began to read a few serious books for the first time in my life. My older brother, who had been reading a lot between air raids on a battered Pacific island, put me on to some convincing criticisms of the American welfare state. Friedrich Hayek, who narrowly escaped the terrible results of unlimited government in Europe, was the scholar whose warning moved me most. His work made me aware that government was a permanent threat to freedom, that big government historically had caused more human misery than it had cured.

I rejected my belief in socialized medicine, deeply embarrassed that I had embraced it in the first place, and took the hard line against government action. I came to believe that government should defend the country, keep the peace —and nothing else. I saw America on the road to socialist ruin. I developed a deep anxiety because so few people shared my sense of onrushing disaster. I swallowed the conservative doctrine whole.* I was, for a time, a conscious and practicing, if not very effective, right-wing extremist. I could imagine no more urgent human mission than to preach the conservative gospel.

In those days, the conservative task seemed simple to me. We needed to alert people to the dangers of big government, then persuade them that we could only have a free society if we strictly limited government's powers. Once we had convinced a working majority, it would be simple enough to pass the laws that would cut government down to its natural size.

I sensed that I needed experience in journalism to play this part effectively, so I got a job writing very minor pieces on economic subjects for *American Affairs*, a business quarterly that soon folded. The editor who hired me was Garet Garrett, who in his day had been a giant among editorial

---

* I even followed its logic to a brief but proud belief in anarchy.

writers, first for the *New York Times* and, in the thirties, for the *Saturday Evening Post*. I was a trial to Mr. Garrett. My tidy ideology often drove him to rage.

One day I turned in a tightly reasoned piece attacking the three-day week that John L. Lewis had decreed for the soft-coal industry. Faithful to conservative gospel, I said that when an industry was losing out in the market, the least able producers and their employees "disappeared." That word shocked Mr. Garrett to the verge of a coronary. He made me go down to the coal fields and visit the disappearing people.

I borrowed an old car and drove through the dreary Kentucky mountain coal towns. Clearly, many people there had been thrown into desperate need by events they couldn't have controlled even if they had understood them. Gaunt and listless men stood in the streets, wondering what they would do if the mines didn't open again. And, my conservative doctrine notwithstanding, these people were not going to disappear. They needed help.

This experience sharply jolted my confidence in pure conservative doctrine, as I then understood it. While I still saw no maturity in the liberal position, which seemed to ignore the awesome power building up in Washington, I now saw for the first time a lack of humanity in my conservative position, which seemed to ignore many of the urgent needs of people.

It seemed that I had, as a citizen, a choice between unacceptable alternatives: (1) I could choke down my conservative belief and urge my Congressman to vote for government programs to help distressed people; or (2) I could close my eyes to human need and urge votes against any government action. Humanity and freedom, as I understood them, seemed to be in permanent conflict.

I continued to propagate the conservative faith, but now sometimes with a feeling in my stomach that there was something missing. Mr. Garrett retired to his farm on the

Tuckahoe River to write books. Probably because my confidence was so badly shaken, I took a less activist role and went to work for a foundation which specialized in encouraging solid conservative scholarship. It was interesting and satisfying work. For several years I succumbed to its fascination, and forgot about the coal miners.

Then, just before he died in 1954, Mr. Garrett woke me up again. He published his most searching book, a sweeping history of the United States called *The American Story* (Regnery, 1954). It did not have a happy ending—for Mr. Garrett believed the American dream was irretrievably down the drain. The dilemma he had earlier posed for me and I had kicked under the rug took on an awesome importance. For, failing to solve it, failing to build a society which was both free and humane, we would, Mr. Garrett predicted, inherit a society which was neither.

I had always read Mr. Garrett uncritically. His pessimism affected me profoundly. It meant the work I was doing was pointless, irrelevant. He was seventy-five; I was twenty-seven. Despair, to an old man, must be very painful; to a young man, it is intolerable. He was soon to die; I had many more years to go.

I began to look for some hope, not at all in a scholarly spirit, but to satisfy an urgent personal need. At first, I didn't have much luck. Then by accident I began a few years ago to grope in the right direction. I found a neglected force at work in America—a force so strong it could resolve the dilemma which had driven Mr. Garrett to despair and me to my anxious search. I found that we Americans once proudly solved most of our common problems outside government, through a rich array of institutions, neither commercial nor governmental, which I am suggesting we call "the independent sector." In the generations when the independent sector had great vitality, human needs were met without adding to the power of government.

In the twentieth century, however, this huge potential

force has fallen behind the surging vitality of private industry and ambitious government. Most people think it is quaint and basically incompetent, too weak and uneven to take serious responsibility in the missile age.

Today, I believe, the independent sector is on the brink of a great renaissance. It can again become the most vital element in our national life. Our most urgent new business is to bring our independent institutions to the full capacity our abundance makes possible. They can do much more of the country's serious business, with more efficiency, precision, and understanding. They can break the bitter stalemate between doctrinaire conservatism and dogmatic liberalism. If we exploit their potential in a tough and practical way, we can reclaim the American dream.

I am tired of angry books about America. This is a hopeful book. It does not say the country is going to hell. It says that perhaps for the first time in her history, America can go wherever she wants to go. And in the process, each citizen may find himself again—by contributing, in his own way, to the creation of the good society.

RECLAIMING
THE AMERICAN
DREAM

1

Resignation, Right and Left

Years ago I knew a hard-core conservative who collected Roosevelt dimes. He was an older man with enough money to buy all the dimes he needed. He needed quite a few. Whenever the angry spirit moved him, he seized a mechanic's ball-peen hammer which he kept handy, and smashed a dime or two.

I thought then he was funny. I know now he was a human tragedy. His basic sentiment was valid. He believed in the ideal of limited government, as most of us do. The belief that we should keep government as small as possible is a deep and essential part of our political tradition. My friend saw government growing at a rate that alarmed him, and in FDR's face he saw the cause of it all. He knew no practical way to work for his ideal; so he swung his hammer in a helpless gesture, to express a real and valid despair.

The conservative frustration doesn't often show itself in such a bizarre and pathetic way. But the defeatism it represents is widespread. The more "respectable" conservatives don't smash dimes. They don't do anything. They think any action is pointless. More and more businessmen, once the proud champions of limited government, are now convinced that ever broader government is inevitable. "As our society has grown more complex," said Henry Ford II in a speech at Yale in 1959, "the government has had to play an ever greater role. . . . That trend is not likely to be reversed." In other words, limited government is impossible in modern America, and we may as well get used to the idea.

Less noticeable, but equally disturbing, is a corresponding frustration among the liberals—at a time when they seem politically invincible. The liberal frustration is of course harder to spot. It is not often advertised by absurdities like dime-smashing. The liberals are in power. They cannot very well picket themselves. They can hardly organize conspiracies against the government they built.

But the liberal restlessness is there. Columnist James Reston writes of "a disenchantment among the liberals." Irving Kristol, writing in the June, 1963, *Harper's* magazine, says:

> In private, nowadays, almost every head of every [federal] department will concede that "things are out of hand"—that between the original idea and the terminal reality there is a long and disillusioning gap.

He quotes one in particular:

> "Everyone knows things have gone wrong, but no one knows how to go about setting them right."

And I have listened in conservative amazement to the bitter cynicism of once militant liberals who have decided to hang up their spurs and watch the world get worse.

This, too, is tragic. The liberal impulse is, like the conservative one, essentially valid. The liberal believes that we should handle public problems promptly and sensibly—that we must be alert to the needs of people. This belief is as vital to the American tradition as is our belief in limited government, and most of us accept it. Yet the liberal spokesmen for this ideal are quietly writing it off. Only when they find a relatively new cause, like Negro rights, on which they have not yet built a history of governmental failure, do they revive for the moment their old élan.

Both the left and the right are abandoning their idealism. Their fringe groups angrily kick the machinery. Their "responsible" leaders are deciding to muddle through a basically hopeless situation. And the American dream fades.

I believe that the conservatives and liberals are frustrated for the same reason. The next two chapters tell why.

---*---

2

Why the Conservatives Can't Win

---*---

Why are the conservatives, spokesmen for the valid American ideal of limited government, giving up that ideal? They are coming to realize they cannot win without a program— without answers for the problems that trouble people. When it seems only government can solve most modern public problems, the conservative can only have a program by advocating bigger government. And that is what he is in business to denounce.

Year after year the liberals have won the public's attention by pointing out urgent public problems. Then they have won public support by proposing specific federal programs intended to solve these problems.

But the conservatives can offer few specific solutions. They have no resources with which to bid against government for public responsibility. They protest without a program, and appear to be rebels without a cause.

This is an awkward stance. "One reason the Democrats appear to be good speakers," says a GOP Congressman, "is that they are always promoting something. It is easier to be enthusiastic when you are advocating some new service. Objecting to things is a difficult position to be in."

The conservatives can win public attention by pointing out the failures of government, but they can offer no specific alternatives. They can only whine about the side effects of big government, as one might complain about the mess left by the firemen who put out a fire.

If they grow weary of the negative position or if they feel threatened by the do-nothing charge, conservatives are tempted to borrow pieces of the opposition's program. "If a Democrat says we need better health," says Republican Senator George Aiken of Vermont, "I am not going to come out for poorer health just to disagree with him." Stuck with a choice between a mulish negativism and grudging agreement, the office-holding conservative often becomes a reluctant "me-too" politician. But this doesn't work either. He violates his own principles, underbids the competition, and loses on both counts.

Lacking a program which does not compromise conservative principle, conservatives can only attack big government. In this battle, they have used every rhetorical, political, parliamentary, and philosophical weapon they can find to assault government. They have tried to repeal it, all at once and in little pieces. They have declared it unconstitutional. They have denounced it as immoral. They have tried to cut off its supply of money and power. They have condemned it as alien to America and tried to deport it. But none of their efforts seem to work.

Consider the conservative crusade against government waste. Researchers camp on the steps of the bureaus and record the waste motion. They add up the number of federal bureaucrats. They count the paper clips. They try to repeal C. Northcote Parkinson's second law: "Expenditure rises to meet income." And so it does. If you give a bureaucrat a dollar, he will spend it. If you tell him he's spending too much on carbon paper, he will thank you for your trouble and spend the savings on filing cabinets.

Nor can you expect civil servants to make government

efficient. No realist expects them to.* (In fact, Charles Kettering once said we should be grateful we don't get as much government as we pay for.) The tireless work of the economizers has some value. It keeps us reminded of the high price we pay for remote control of public service. But waste is only a symptom of a deeper trouble. You can't beat a leviathan with a red pencil. This form of conservative protest, like the other protests, is vain.

Conservatives have tried to stop big government by starving it. "If we want to stop the Washington spenders from bankrupting our nation, socializing our economy, and reducing us to slavery," wrote Dan Smoot in 1957, "we must cut off the money supply from the Washington spenders." Smoot is one of many who preach that we can't afford big government. To pay its bills with taxes will cripple us economically; to pay them with debt will bring landslide inflation.

But the starvation strategy ignores the fundamental force behind government's growth. Bills pile up because government has a lot to do. Since it takes responsibility, it needs money. Much as it might like to, Congress can't give an agency a job to do and then hold back the funds to pay the bills.

Conservatives have tried to fight with philosophy. They say big government is wrong. But Franklin Roosevelt taught liberals how to turn back this verbal offensive. "This country," he said of the Depression, "was faced with a condition, not a theory." The programs of modern liberalism grew out of that condition. "What excited Roosevelt," wrote Robert Sherwood in the official biography, "was not grand eco-

* The habit of blaming big government on its employees has persuaded many conservatives that government workers are a special breed put here on earth to bedevil people. Novelist Ayn Rand lists them among "the spoilers." However, most bureaucrats are earnest citizens who want to win recognition by serving the public. To attack them as a class may win a few votes, but never so many as the bureaucracy itself delivers to the other side.

nomic and political theory but concrete achievements that people could touch and see and use."

Franklin D. Roosevelt, Jr., looking back today in candid admiration of his father, says, "The New Deal was never thought out. It hardly had any philosophy, except one principle: that government has the obligation to step in when the individual can't handle basic economic problems." Conservatives have tried in vain to oppose pragmatic programs with philosophical arguments.

Conservatives have sought support by contending that big government is dangerous, leading in time to tyranny. In 1944 the University of Chicago Press published a brilliant book by Friedrich A. Hayek called *The Road to Serfdom*. Hayek used Germany, which he knew well, to prove his point, demonstrating that the Nazi terror grew out of the Bismarck welfare state. The book, with apologies to Professor Hayek, said this:

> If you give government a lot to do, you have to give it the power to do it. As this power adds up, it grows harder and harder to control. In time, in spite of its benign origin, this power can be turned back hideously on the very people who give it up in the first place.

Hayek frightened Americans. Ever since our Constitutional Convention, and visibly since the Civil War, the country had become more and more centralized. In the Depression, and in World War II, the centralization trend seemed to have become total. You could smell the danger everywhere.

Hayek's book no doubt helped bring about the change in political weather which elected President Eisenhower in 1952. By then, conservatives had seized the Hayek thesis and made it their battle cry. They fought every sign of federal action as another milestone on the road to serfdom.

This campaign, like others before it, may have done conservatism more harm than good. Because whether you believe the Hayek thesis or not, you know what it left in the public unconscious: a feeling that big government is dangerous medicine—so it probably works.

The conservative's campaign against big government has been driven onward, and then repeatedly frustrated, because the public so often seems to be on his side. The average American doesn't like big government. He doesn't like taxes. He's afraid of debt and inflation. He favors free enterprise. He knows that government wastes money.

The polls make these beliefs clear. In a 1962 California poll, conducted by Belden Associates for the Purdue Research Foundation, 62 per cent of the people believed it would be better if private business did more of what the government now does. Only 21 per cent took the other side. No less than 58 per cent believed it would be better for state and local governments to do more of the things the federal government is doing; only 24 per cent thought responsibility should flow the other way.

Such evidence seemed to support the myth that has warped conservative strategy for two decades. The silent majority of adults, we conservatives told each other, were with us. We had only to give them a chance to express their loyalty—a choice. The 1964 Presidential vote demolished this notion. Conservatives know now that there just isn't much of a silent conservative vote, and the myth no longer provides any comfort.

It never should have. Though the average American opposes big government, he also believes that we have more and more problems which only the government wants to tackle. So he applauds the conservative rhetoric and supports the liberal program.*

T. H. White, in his best-selling *The Making of a Presi-*

---

* So Goldwater did well when he wasn't a Presidential candidate, and poorly when he was.

dent, 1960 (Atheneum, 1961), put the conservative dilemma eloquently:

> The Democratic philosophy, usually unspoken but quite clear nonetheless, is that government is there to be used as an instrument of action. . . .
> The Republican philosophy is entirely different, clearer in metaphysical terms yet murkier in political expression. It is the belief, deep down, that each citizen bears a responsibility in private life and in community life as great or greater than the responsibility of government to shape that life and community. Part of the Republican tragedy in recent years has been the inability of its thinkers to articulate this philosophy clearly enough to draw political conclusions and programs from it.

The trials of 1964 put the challenge directly to the conservatives. The job was not to change their "image," as the public relations experts always urge, but to confront the real and tangible crisis in the nation's life. A well-known commentator, Eric Sevareid, writing on the Goldwater campaign, summed it up precisely:

> When he [Goldwater] suggests that family relief in the vast, sprawling Harlems of America can be turned over to the lodges, unions, private charities and relatives of the indigent—when he says these things he is not solving the problems, he is wishing them away. Yet he is perfectly correct when he reports that the problems of our time and our society are not being solved as matters are going. And in this profound frustration must lie the key to Goldwater's large following. It is not half so much a movement with a program as one with a protest. It is a desperate, confused protest against a desperately confused new world of human living rising around us at home and abroad. Millions

have simply given up trying to understand it, let alone cope with it.

The demand for a conservative alternative is explicit. Trying to size up the meaning of the noisy renaissance of conservative political action, T George Harris, writing in *Look* (July 16, 1963), put it in simple terms:

> The liberal vision of the future . . . inspired men to specific action toward a better society. Now [liberalism] has grown fat with success and stale in its addiction to federal pills for all ills. What is the right's alternative?

The conservative can't, it seems, answer this call. He has no program. He knows now he can't win without a program. Yet he knows of no honorable way to create one. He is left to talk to himself about his principles, principles which the public already largely supports. And the liberals, because they have a program of sorts, gain votes at a time when the public is least enthusiastic about what they advocate.

3

Why the Liberals Can't Win

As the conservative is losing his battle because he has no program at all, the liberal is coming to a different dead end. He finds out he can't achieve his ideal—the ideal of a society that solves social problems—with the program he has.

To be sure, the liberal always has a program. But as government has emerged as the only agency which seems able to cope with modern public problems, the liberal program is always a government program. The belief in federal action has thus become the central commandment of today's liberal creed, and hence of the dominant political leadership. Irving Kristol, in the *Harper's* article quoted in Chapter 1, put it precisely:

> The liberal community—i.e., the teachers, the journalists, the civil servants, the trade unionists, the leaders of minority groups, etc.—envisages the welfare state as *the one institution* through which it can exercise power and authority over the nation's affairs. [Italics added]

Liberals play limitless expensive variations on their single federal theme. They express their impatience for a better society only through the channel of government action. They see only one bottle of pills on the shelf, aspirin made in Washington, and they prescribe it for all social ailments.

In recent years, however, a rising skepticism has begun to infect this federal faith. Honest, well-intentioned men who once championed the federal alphabet agencies have had time to measure promise against performance. And they see a widening gap between what government says it can do and what it gets done.

Some years ago John Dos Passos, once a militant liberal and author of the hotly emotional *USA* novels of the thirties, took part in a seminar on public policy. Sitting on the sidelines, I watched Dos Passos when the talk turned to the issue of how much responsibility the government should take in human affairs.

"One of the reasons I voted for Roosevelt in 1932 was that the capitalists were polluting the streams," he said. "One of the things that gave me pause about the choice, only eight years later, was that the capitalists were still polluting the streams."

Others have come to similar, if less colorful, conclusions. Scholar after scholar has been surprised by the record of failure in federal programs. The federal urban renewal program is becoming the classic example. After sixteen years of experiment in urban renewal, there is only one honest conclusion: the federal effort has flopped. It hurts the poor it promises to help and holds back improvement in private housing for poor people.

Some observers began to put the evidence together in the late fifties. By October, 1961, Professor Martin Meyerson, then Director of the Joint Center for Urban Studies of M.I.T. and Harvard, took aim at the "peculiar mystique" around urban renewal: "As soon as people begin facing the implications of urban renewal, I think that the support will wither and turn in considerable measure to hostility. . . ."

Jane Jacobs, author of *The Death and Life of Great American Cities* (Random House, 1961), concluded after many months of careful study that the quality of human life in the new concrete city-scapes was often worse than that in the asphalt jungles the government had massively "renewed."

It remained only for Columbia University's Martin Anderson to deliver the overall statistical study, published in book form as *The Federal Bulldozer* (M.I.T. Press, 1964). Anderson, trained in the liberal tradition, could hardly believe his own figures. Urban renewal projects, advertised as help for the poor, make it harder for low- and middle-income families to find homes. On the other hand, the private developers have been rapidly upgrading the quality of houses which poor people can afford.

Anderson's devastating summary appears on page 197 of *Bulldozer*:

> Virtually all of this [progress] was accomplished by private construction, rehabilitation, and demolition efforts that resulted from the investment of massive amounts of private funds in housing that was in no way connected with the federal urban renewal program.

As it goes in urban renewal, so it goes in many other federal efforts, old and now. Economist Norton E. Long of Brandeis, in his 1965 monograph "The Reduction of Poverty," bitterly attacks present welfare policies as a system that merely "removes the eyesore of hopeless poverty from middle class view." He struck hardest at anti-poverty gestures that do not solve the poor men's true need—for wage-paying work.

We are in danger of drifting into cosmetic cures. . . . We already have a model for how an affluent society might deal with surplus people—the way we deal with surplus grain. What we do with grain is store it and keep it off the market so it won't hurt the price. We do the same with the poor—we store them in slums and public housing to keep them off the labor market so they won't reduce wage rates or otherwise compete in the only way they can.

The difference between people and grain, however, is that if you store grain it merely rots; if you store people they rot and reproduce, and the children that they reproduce are brought up and educated in conditions in which it is likely that many of them will rot too. The evil with the agricultural storage policy for dealing with people is thus not alone that of keeping needed resources from meeting human wants but from creating conditions by which the evil multiplies rather than diminishes.

The government's grain storage program doesn't work either. The architects of the farm price subsidy never dreamed, on their most restless nights, that the cost would multiply to its present level. Here the government's record is not only bad but perverse. In the name of helping the helpless, its programs turn into subsidies for the rich. Eighty per cent of the commodity subsidies now go to the one million farmers whose average income exceeds $9,500, while the other 20 per cent of the government money seeps thinly down to the remaining two and a half million poor farmers.

Other government programs now draw fire from surprising quarters. David Lilienthal, former Chairman of TVA and of the Atomic Energy Commission, a father figure among liberal administrators, has studied at first-hand the effect of federal scientific programs, which now monopolize better than two thirds of our scientific manpower. In his book *Change, Hope and the Bomb* (Princeton University Press, 1963), Lilienthal sounded a warning to all scientists:

Scientists have—unwittingly, perhaps, at first—been in part responsible for diluting the spirit of independent inquiry that is the very core of science, by becoming uncritical advocates and even lobbyists for various huge "programmatic" technical enterprises. . . .

Now scientists are "organization men" . . . in many cases the independent and humble search for new truths about nature has become confused with the bureaucratic impulse to justify expenditure and to see that next year's budget is bigger than last's.

To be a scientist at all may come to mean being a scientist who is in a program that would not exist without tax-fund support and public—that is, political —goals.

Liberalism, as expressed in a generation of federal programs, is now failing. An interviewer asked a Midwestern college student why conservatism draws new interest on campus. "People are frustrated with the failures of liberalism," came the answer. "There is a growing realization that liberal policies don't work."

But liberals have to live with this sorry record. They have to live with silliness, as when a bubble-gum manufacturer is indicted as a dangerous monopolist. They have to live with power applied without mercy, as when government agents seize and sell an Amish farmer's team because he has religious scruples against social security. They have to live with moss-backed regulatory agencies like the Interstate Commerce Commission, which has turned large parts of a proud industry into a sick cartel that often rattles the cup for subsidy.

And so, naturally, we find a growing uneasiness in the liberal household. We see some of the symptoms of this uneasiness in the liberal's growing impatience with dissent, his tendency to deal with opponents by epithet rather than argument, and in a general listlessness in a movement once remarkable for its spirit. Worst of all, perhaps, the liberals have left themselves open to the cruel joke that says they love humanity but hate people.

How do we account for the mounting failure of the liberal program? Apparently, government action grows less and less appropriate as human affairs grow more and more complicated. Walter Lippmann discussed this in his classic *The Good Society* (Little, Brown, 1937):

> It is generally supposed that the increasing complexity of the social order requires an increasing direction from officials. My own view is, rather, as affairs become more intricate, more extended in time and space, more involved and inter-related, overhead direction by officials of the state has to become simpler, less intensive, less direct, more general. . . . Thus it is, I believe, a maxim of human association that the complexity of policy as distinguished from law must be inversely proportionate to the complexity of affairs. For, while a few things can be directed much, many things can be administered only a little.*

Philosopher Paul Goodman says something similar in a much more recent book. In the first lines of *People or Personnel* (Random House, 1965), he writes:

> Throughout society, the centralizing style of organization has been pushed so far as to become ineffectual, economically wasteful, humanly stultifying, and ruinous to democracy.

But this explanation of the failure of the liberal program gives no comfort to the disenchanted liberal. Government

---

* It must be said that Mr. Lippmann has changed his agile mind about a lot of things in the unsettling years since 1937, probably including this sound insight.

still seems the only agency willing and able to tackle modern public problems. So the veteran liberal finds himself imprisoned. He can either abandon his idealism, as many now do, or he can continue to promote big government, desperately hoping that the next federal program may somehow be better than the last.

4

That Was the Dream That Was

And so the spokesmen for two valid American ambitions stop at separate dead ends. Neither liberals nor conservatives can get what they want for America. In mutual frustration they spend most of their energy fighting each other. The conservative points scornfully to the failures of the liberal program; the liberal decries the conservative's inhumanity.

Yet neither rejects the other's central idealism. Few conservatives oppose the notion of the good society. Few liberals think bigger government is a good thing.

The strategy of each side inspires the other's total opposition. Liberals, conditioned in years of political success, can serve their ideal only by expanding government to meet every new need; conservatives can serve their ideal only by shrinking government. The two courses of action collide. One position can advance only at the other's expense. So our political discussion has been, for several years, little more than a daily barrage of bitter invective. Debate cannot bring adjustment. Both sides retreat to prepared positions in hardened ideology.

"Everyone has to be concerned with the apparent conflict between welfare and freedom," believes John Burkhart, president of The College Life Insurance Company and a conservative businessman who works hard on welfare needs in his home state of Indiana. "Our country has become excessively—you might say obsessively—polarized around the liberal and conservative positions. The underlying issues remain unexamined, communication scanty, common action a vanished hope."

It was not always so. For a long time it seemed that the free society and the good society could be realized together in America. This, I think, was the American dream. And for a hundred years and more, it worked.

We wanted, from the beginning, a free society, free in the sense that every man was his own supervisor and the architect of his own ambitions. So our founders took pains to design a government with limited power, and then carefully scattered the forces which could control it.

We wanted as well, with equal fervor, a good society— a humane, responsible society in which helping hands reached out to people in honest distress, in which common needs were met freely and fully. In pursuit of this ambition, Americans used remarkable imagination. We created a much wider variety of new institutions for this purpose than we built to insure political freedom. As a frontier people, accustomed to interdependence, we developed a genius for solving common problems. People joined together in bewildering combinations to found schools, churches, opera houses, co-ops, hospitals, to build bridges and canals, to help the poor. To see a need was, more often than not, to promote a scheme to meet it better than had ever been done before.

The American dream was coming true. Each part of it supported another part. We were free because we limited the power of government. We prospered because we were free.* We built a good society because our prosperity yielded surplus energy which we put directly to work to meet human needs. Thus, we didn't need much government, and because we didn't, we stayed uniquely free. A sort of supportive circle, or spiral, was working for us.

The part of the system least understood, then as now, was the network of non-governmental institutions which served public needs. They did not leave an easy trace for historians to follow. They did not depend on noisy political debate for approval, nor did civil servants have to keep very detailed records of what they did. We will look into the special character of these institutions in the next chapter, but for the moment notice only that they played a significant role. They were not limited to Christmas-basket charity. They took on almost any public job and so became the principal way Americans got things done.

For years the leading colleges and universities were created by the churches. Hospitals began in a variety of ways, and in the era after the Civil War, under Clara Barton's leadership, they blossomed into today's major system of independent institutions. Many of our giant commercial firms, notably in insurance and mutual savings, grew out of early self-help organizations.

Urgent problems filled the agenda of public business in early America. Citizens, acting on their own, took the heavy load. Local and state government took most of what was left. We rarely needed the federal government, a distant thing to the frontiersman. We limited government, not only because people knew its limitations and wanted it limited, but because we left little for it to do.†

---

* Our prosperity was in part blind luck. No economist stood by the Constitutional Convention to tell the delegates how this or that political arrangement might raise or lower the gross national product. We became most prosperous simply because we were most free, and we built a commercial order that would have confounded Adam Smith.

† You may consider this interpretation of our history as simplistic, or perhaps simple-minded. But this is not the book, nor am I the historian, to provide the elaborate documentation of the detailed evo-

America's unique approach arose, as did much of our history, from the special demands of the frontier. Without built-in class lines or tired traditions to say who was responsible for what, the public business became everybody's urgent business. Each new frontier outpost became another New World experiment. We created new forms as we needed them to handle new problems. As the nation grew, so did the magnificent variety of non-governmental devices and organizations.

But a new century brought radical changes in the nature of our public problems. Air pollution did not disturb people when they owned no cars and few factories, nor was there need of rural electrification when there wasn't any electricity. Nor did the prospect of technological unemployment puzzle people when there wasn't much technology.

Now we see a mounting agenda of problems so large and complex that only government, the largest single force in sight, seems big enough to handle them.*

Chronic unemployment infects Appalachia. We face a large and growing problem of juvenile delinquency. Thousands of people willing and able to work can't find the jobs to match their skills. We discriminate against Negroes, thereby conditioning them to expect little of themselves. Our schools need more classrooms and more teachers. Many of our rivers are sewers. We need more parks, the lungs of our citified society. We need to restore the rotting cores of our towns and cities. Our children get dirty pictures in the mail. Helpless, lonely old people stare at walls in dreary rooming houses and look through dirty windows

---

lution of our non-governmental institutions. My purpose is to start, rather than finish, a search for better understanding of this forgotten tradition.

   * The list of big jobs rises naturally as our standard of expectations rises. This is as it should be. "The absolutely exasperating thing about America," says an admiring British diplomat, "is that it expects the impossible from itself." This old habit can destroy us only if we fail to find the right way to act on it.

upon a society that will pay them to rot in silence but won't take time to find a place for them. Traffic chokes our highways. Commuters feel the railroads dying under them. Too often we see dreadful pap on television. We walk the city streets at night in fear.

Confounded by such a staggering agenda, the private citizen has come to feel that technical progress creates public problems faster than it solves them—so many that only government seems big enough to work on them. Professor John K. Galbraith has put this conventional belief into a sort of litany: ". . . functions accrue to the state because, as a purely technical matter, there is no alternative to public management."

This attitude was born of the Depression. Black Friday 1929 struck down American confidence. In our little town the mill shut down, and one in four of our neighbors had no work and no prospects. The months dragged on. The national mood was one of total defeat and despair. We elected Roosevelt and Congress gave him a blank check. People were ready to accept anything. The Depression trauma ran deep and touched nearly everyone. It marked the end of automatic confidence in our traditional way of doing things.

That confidence has never been completely restored. Our habit of sending difficult problems to Washington quickly became almost a reflex. A one-way flow of responsibility to the federal government, begun by Depression remedies, has continued and gained speed. In less than thirty years the government has nearly cornered the market for new public responsibility.

This rather sudden disappearance of any evident alternative to government action profoundly affected our national life. It broke the spiral I referred to earlier. The liberal and the conservative could no longer realize their ideals together, as once they had. The conservative was thrown into his uncomfortable, negative posture; the liberal was frozen in his pro-government attitude. The American dream "as a purely technical matter" seems to be no longer practical.

The American people, torn between conflicting goals, are confused and uncertain. They contradict themselves. They speak against "socialism" but vote for programs which they define as socialism. Norman Thomas, the genial old Socialist, points out: "Along with the acceptance of the welfare state in practice is the curious theoretical insistence on an old-fashioned, non-existent, laissez faire, competitive free enterprise as basic to the American way of life."

Richard Rovere wrote in the September, 1962, issue of *Harper's* magazine: "though [the people] tend to think poorly of the 'welfare state' as a principle of organization," they support it anyway.

This is America's dilemma. We can make no acceptable choice on public issues. Humanity and freedom seem now to be in permanent conflict. So we begin mournfully to resign ourselves to a cut-rate version of the American dream. Just as man's youthful idealism gives way in time to a "mature" sense of what seems practical, the American dream seems less and less like a vision of present reality or the emergent future.

The frustration of the conservatives and the frustration of the liberals add up to the total frustration of the average citizen. For he is, in one sense, neither conservative nor liberal and, in another sense, he is both. We now ask him to split himself, or take a side that cannot command his full allegiance, or dodge the issue by allegiance to a personality. And so he cares less and less who wins.

✳

5

The Rediscovery
of Independent Action

✳

Overwhelmed by the problems of the Depression, we suddenly turned most of our attention to Washington. In so doing, we unconsciously turned our backs on the tradition of non-governmental action which had held our dream together for 150 years. We suddenly forgot this tradition, dropped it from our conversation, almost as if it had never existed.

It quickly became fashionable to speak of American life in terms of only two "sectors": the public sector, which is a prejudicial euphemism for government, and the private sector, which is profit-seeking commerce. We leave out the third sector in our national life, the one which is neither governmental nor commercial. We ignore the institutions which once played such a decisive part in the society's vibrant growth. By assuming a major role in meeting public needs, thus leaving less to government, this third sector once made it possible for us to build a humane society and a free society together.

This important third force deserves a name. It is a distinct, identifiable part of American life, not just a misty area between commerce and government. I have come to call it "the independent sector." After some years of work among the people and organizations operating in this sector, no other word seems to express its unique, intrepid character as well as the word independent.

When I first began to sense the importance of the independent sector, I discovered the best analysis of its function had been written by Alexis de Tocqueville, the young French aristocrat who came to our young nation in the 1830s. His monumental *Democracy in America* provided such prophetic insight into the inner workings of this country that generations of scholars have been forced to argue with his conclusions or accept them. They cannot ignore him. Few have improved on his work.

Tocqueville saw the American impulse to act independently on the public business as our most remarkable trait. He marveled not so much at our economic success and our political machinery as at our tendency to handle public business directly and spontaneously. He wrote that our "associations"—his word for independent institutions— were the key to a social system that he deeply admired. He saw the vigor, ingenuity, and enterprise of these associations, and sensed the boundless potential of their work. Note these lines from Volume II, Second Book, Chapter V (Vintage edition):

> The Americans make associations to give entertainments, to found seminaries, to build inns, to construct churches, to diffuse books, to send missionaries to the antipodes; in this manner they found hospitals, prisons and schools. . . . Whenever at the head of some new undertaking you see the government in France, or a man of rank in England, in the United States you will be sure to find an association.
>
> Only those associations . . . in civil life without reference to political objects are here referred to. The political associations that exist in the United

States are only a single feature in the midst of an immense assemblage of associations in that country.

Nothing . . . is more deserving of our attention. . . . The political and industrial associations strike us forcibly; but the others elude our observation because we have never seen anything of the kind. . . . they are as necessary . . . as the former and perhaps more so. . . . the progress of the rest depends on the progress it has made.

So Tocqueville, the most acute observer of our past, saw three sectors in America: a then primitive commercial sector, a carefully limited government sector, and, most important, a unique and vigorous independent sector.

Yet, as we have seen, the popular writers of our day don't even mention Tocqueville's "associations." People now talk only of the public and the private sectors. The habit is almost as pronounced among conservatives as among liberals, and it seriously limits the vision and action of both. Businessmen speak of America as a free enterprise system, as if this were a total description of our way of life. We do, of course, organize our commercial sector, by and large, on free enterprise principles, but free enterprise isn't an all-purpose social system. To try to make it so is to push it beyond its limits, and thus invite government to do whatever business can't do.

The omission of the independent sector also distorts our discussions of our governmental system. We speak of America as a democracy or a republic. We mean only that the people elect the officials who run the government sector. But political democracy is only a fraction of our heritage. Except where the vote is denied, voting is perhaps one of the least effective acts of the responsible citizen. But to describe America as a democracy implies that voting represents a citizen's total responsibility.

America has been unique, not because we organize our

commercial sector on free enterprise lines or because we elect those who control government, although we talk about these things the most. We have been unique because another sector, clearly distinct from the other two, has, in the past, borne a heavy load of public responsibility.

But since the Depression, we have thought the use of the independent sector's usefulness to be limited, and we find many experts writing off the sector of society Tocqueville thought we needed most. "The myth persisted for a time," says Dean Quadri of the New York School of Social Work, "that private charity could carry the burden of relief." But, he continues, "The individual who prefers to take a basket of food to a 'worthy' family bears the same relationship to modern social welfare as the individual artisan, painstakingly spinning his wool . . . bears to the American economy."

Michael Harrington, whose book *The Other America* (Penguin, 1963) seemed to inspire the federal poverty program, writes: "It is a noble sentiment to argue that private moral responsibility expressing itself through charitable contributions should be the main instrument of attacking poverty. The only problem is that such an approach does not work."

So, what can the independent sector do in modern America? Not, some experts think, very much. I once heard a prominent Columbia economist give these examples: ". . . maintenance of a dog cemetery, or the maintenance of bird sanctuaries, or the climbing of Mt. Everest." His clinching judgment: "Air-tight examples of this sort are increasingly hard to find."

So we have quietly dropped the independent sector from important public conversation. No one protests when Professor Galbraith writes a best-seller about the sectors of *The Affluent Society* and ignores the third sector entirely.

The loss is more fundamental than we know. We dam the wellspring of social initiative. Almost exactly a century after Tocqueville found independent action to be the key to our future, another well-known foreign observer, Gunnar Myrdal, wrote in *An American Dilemma* (Harper & Row, 1944):

> They [the American masses] are accustomed to being static and receptive. . . . They do not know how to cooperate and how to pool risks for a common goal. They do not meet much. They do not organize. They do not speak for themselves.

And in his more recent book *Challenge to Affluence* (Pantheon, 1963), Myrdal goes on to show the consequence:

> The citizen's participation in public life, taken in its broadest terms, is lower in America than generally in countries that are similar to it in basic values.

In other words, what Tocqueville found unique and remarkable in America, our proud involvement in public business, Myrdal finds remarkably absent. Myrdal's report is part fact, I believe, and part self-confirming myth. But in 1952, the University of Michigan Survey Research Center found that 62.8 per cent of heads of households did not take part in any formal group or organization; only 10 per cent were active in two or more.

You may find the result in the words of other willing pall-bearers for the American dream. Says Britain's D. W. Brogan in his *American Aspects* (Harper & Row, 1965):

> It is inevitable, even if regrettable, that the unique character of the American and of the American experiment is over.

So we hear glib assertions that the independent sector is gone forever and the dream it supported is finished. Though we heed their warnings, we need not resign ourselves to their grim prophesy. Our confidence in the independent sector was badly shaken by the Depression. No one doubts that. But the independent impulse is not dead in America. Far from it. Because we don't look for it, we don't see it—we fail to exploit its potential. But when you become involved in a specific effort, you begin to sense you are dealing with a great and growing latent power.

A little more than a year ago, at the University Club in New York, I sat in on an off-the-record meeting of business leaders, economists, and university administrators whose purpose was to discuss unemployment and the fear that, with automation, it would stay high or rise. The meeting had been called by the National Association of Manufacturers and was attended by top representatives from five other major business associations.

We quickly agreed the unemployment situation was acute and had to be solved. We all knew the federal government, already pushing the poverty program, wanted to launch a bigger and bigger effort. No one there wanted federal action that would expand forever. And this group, which knew as well as anybody what would work in the market place and what wouldn't, believed that the federal agencies would institutionalize the problem rather than solve it.

For a time, the conversation hung up at this point. We saw an important public problem emerging. The only real prospect: government would attack it with doubtful weapons.

Then one of the younger men got down to specifics. "How many jobs are we talking about?" he asked. One of the economists said the figures weren't clear, but a million jobs would be a good operating assumption for the moment.

"Now suppose," the young man continued, "all the non-governmental groups in America figured out what they could do to solve the problem and did it. Couldn't we lick it? *There has to be a better way to solve this problem than to send it to Washington.*" The next three hours filled me with hope. We had heard the question in a way that forced a new kind of response. The young man challenged us to think positively—to explore the forgotten potential of independent action.

The head of a great business research association pointed out that we have data on the unemployed but not on job vacancies. To match the unemployed talent against job opportunities, present and future, his staff could probably develop a "national job inventory." They had techniques, he believed, to lick that part of the problem.

Another research specialist picked up from there, offered to develop better data on the unemployed and their unused talents. Still another research chief resolved to focus research on investment opportunities in labor-intense industries like the service trades. If business looks upon the unemployed as a resource rather than a nuisance, he pointed out, it can surely develop new opportunities for people who now seem unemployable.

And so it went. One idea lighted another like a string of firecrackers. Then, in the days after the meeting, people began to move. The outfits which took on the toughest jobs became the most deeply involved. The NAM threw its staff and members into what it called Project STEP, for Solutions to Employment Problems. NAM Executive Vice-President Bennett Kline blanketed the U.S. business community with questionnaires designed to find those who knew how to recruit and train otherwise unemployable people. Hundreds of replies flowed back, forming a bank of technical know-how on the subject. Kline's staff checked out the most promising replies, distributed the results to other companies and communities. Pushing for action on the new information, he scheduled regional seminars to teach businessmen this practical art. Still, he wanted to set up a hard test. So he selected five cities in which to launch pilot projects for full-scale attacks upon unemployment by business and community agencies. If the pilot cities failed, he would try other methods. He also went beyond the present unemployment list into the long-term need to further upgrade talent at each level of a labor force facing ever new technology. He set up a major study of industry's education and training programs with the view to expanding the most successful ones. He was amused to discover a new difficulty he had not heard of before: the Ph.D. dropout, based on the failure of promising graduate students to find ways to combine work and study.

"We have seen enough," Kline decided a few months later, "to know that somebody, somewhere, has found a solution to every imaginable employment problem. Our job is to put the solutions into wider use."

As the idea began to percolate throughout the business community, new groups responded or expanded their previous efforts. The volunteer list of activists ranged from the National Industrial Conference Board and the Chamber of Commerce to Harvard's Graduate School of Business and the League of Women Voters. Some of the original ideas turned sour, but they were replaced by dozens more. A data-processing firm with a nation-wide computer network joined a group of employment agencies to test a quick-reporting national job inventory; a business foundation put up thousands to finance this important test.

As this work now gets well under way, each move turns up more useful resources that the independent sector can tap. Perhaps in reaction, the *Wall Street Journal* did a national survey on business investment in education and on-the-job training. Each year, companies and workers invest a minimum of $4.5 billion in working knowledge— or a maximum of $20 billion, depending on how you try to count the countless efforts. With such a huge base to build upon—far greater than the federal effort and better geared to each need—calculated expansion of the best projects will pay off in millions of new and better job placements.

Just how much will be done through this collaboration of independent and business action depends on how effectively the NAM and other private organizations can mobilize and lever the commercial sector into action. The total results will never be known. By its nature, the independent sector can set off chain reactions that are too far-reaching to keep books on. But if the U.S. economy defies the dire predictions about rising unemployment in an automation era, you and I can give part of the credit to a group of men who worried around a table at the University Club on a hot summer day.

They started to uncover the vast, idle capacities of individuals and institutions to act directly and freely on public problems. They began, just a little, to rediscover the part of America which once had been her unique and proudest feature.

6

The Independent
Sector

When you push back the curtain that has strangely hidden the independent sector from the public eye, one surprise follows another. You notice dozens of agencies that serve you daily. The sector's dimensions are fantastic, its raw strength awesome.

In a sharpened awareness, people who think government is the only source of welfare suddenly discover new facts. A university faculty member, for instance, will realize that he, along with 180,000 colleagues in 1,300 leading schools, gets his medical insurance and pension rights from Teachers Insurance and Annuity Association, a national independent agency that out-performs state retirement plans. TIAA stands as a visible giant among independent institutions, but many of our independent agencies long ago blended into the social landscape. Under the spotlight, they take on a variety of forms so rich they can be illustrated but never fully described.

Sometimes the independent impulse shows itself in humble, simple ways, as when our new neighbors brought a pot of soup and offered to sit with the baby when we moved into our tract house in San Mateo.

Sometimes it shows itself boldly and professionally, as when the National Foundation for Infantile Paralysis set out to conquer polio with dimes—and did it.

Sometimes the independent sector deals with small pleasures, as when my wife's Garden Guild attends to the floral decorations at our church.

But often it deals with grave problems, as when Stanford Research Institute designs weapons systems and strategy on which our defense depends.

Sometimes independent action is impulsive, as when thousands of Americans mailed $600,000 to Dallas Patrolman J. D. Tippit's grief-stricken wife and $78,000 to the assassin's stunned young widow. But often it is highly systematic, as when the Ford Foundation coaches colleges and universities in the complexities of long-range capital planning.

Sometimes the independent sector does menial, dirty work, as when volunteer hospital aides empty the bedpans and bandage the oozing sores of patients in hospitals all across the country. But often it does what is most gracious and aesthetic, as when the Guggenheim family builds a magnificent museum or citizens in Pittsburgh sponsor the display of the work of their local artists in the foyers of business and public places.

Sometimes the independent sector does silly things. The Air Mail from God Mission used to drop Protestant tracts from airplanes on the Catholic villages in rural Mexico. But as often, independent institutions work with great sophistication, as when the Sloan-Kettering Institute develops an effective chemotherapy for some forms of cancer and doggedly continues to search for better ways to fight this killer.

Sometimes independent action shows itself in ugly, perverse ways, as when the Ku Klux Klan organizes a vigilante force to terrorize Negro Americans or the Minutemen drill grimly in their cellars. But more often, it moves with a soul-stirring magnificence, as when Dr. Tom Dooley hurriedly raised money to finish his hospital in the Laotian jungle before cancer drained his life away.

Sometimes independent action is highly individual. Leo Seligman of Memphis, who learned about prison life the hard way in a Nazi concentration camp, has met 786 parolees at prison gates in Tennessee with bus fare, lunch, and a helping hand. But it is often highly organized. The Boy Scouts can tell you to the penny how much it takes to set up a troop.

Independent action is sometimes almost invisible. Did you know more private than public land is available free for camping? (And California's Redwood Association has launched a program among lumbermen to provide still more public camp sites on private land.) Sometimes the independent sector screams for attention, as when mass media annually harangue us to contribute to United Fund campaigns.

Independent action is sometimes frivolous, as when groups are organized for treks in classic cars or to learn to be amateur clowns. But it is sometimes in deadly earnest, as when the business leaders of Dallas jointly acted to integrate the schools and privately owned public facilities of their city.

Sometimes the independent sector provides our luxuries. Most of our opera houses are independent institutions, and independent symphonies provide cultural leaven in more than twelve hundred American communities. Sometimes it provides desperate necessities, as when Salvation Army centers give a meal and a bed to men who would otherwise sleep hungry in the street.

Sometimes independent action is inane, as when a group sought to make Alcatraz a museum of horrors, its cells permanently occupied by wax replicas of the prison's famous inmates. But sometimes it is forward-looking and ingenious, as when the Upjohn Foundation combined with Systems Development Corporation to work out a national system of finding and communicating job opportunities to the jobless.

The independent sector is a kaleidoscope of human action. It takes a thousand forms and works in a million ways. And a tremendous raw strength undergirds its rich variety. Welded into our national life at every level, it functions at any moment when a person or group acts directly to serve others. The independent sector is, to begin with, 190 million individuals in 50 million families—who do not limit their lives to pay-earning work (the personal commercial sector) or occasional trips to the voting booth (the personal government sector). We are the richest, best educated, most ingenious people in the history of the world. Seventy-one million of us in the labor force produce goods and services worth $630 billion annually. We channel much of this wealth—plus talent and energy not counted by the GNP figures—through the independent sector.

Life magazine noted in its January 4, 1963, issue that eight million American families (twenty-seven million people) have after-tax incomes of $10,000 or more. "In no previous society," *Life* commented, "has there ever been a privileged class of such dimensions, or one that has so swiftly emerged. . . . What kind of social chemistry is set in motion when we double or triple the number of the talented, ambitious and privileged?"

The family's ability to help itself and others outside the family group is great and growing. In 1959, American families provided food and shelter worth $4.5 billion to relatives living with them. In 1959, the Survey Research Center at the University of Michigan figured 53 million families contributed more than $6 billion to churches, $2 billion to charity, and $7 billion to other individuals. In the past five years, especially in the past two, the giving habit has grown so abundantly that the figures are difficult to estimate.

Americans have developed a rich variety of organizations through which they arrange their time, energy, and ingenuity for public service. First of all, our churches. In America 320,000 churches with 118 million members own assets worth $15 billion.

In addition, a hundred thousand voluntary welfare groups, and no one knows how many informal neighborhood, college and community groups, have organized to tutor underprivileged children or plan to eliminate slums, discuss Great Books and a thousand more duties.

Six thousand private foundations worth $14.5 billion finance activities ranging from the intensive study of the habits of orang-utans to regional economic development in poor nations.

Hundreds of fraternal and service organizations, with over thirty-six million members, not only march in parades but also send needy youngsters to college and look for other ways to help their communities and their nation.* Kiwanis, Rotary, Civitan and Lions Clubs, as well as Chambers of Commerce and the zestful Jaycees, take on ever bigger jobs.

Hundreds of labor unions, with about thirteen million members, not only bargain with the boss but also run hospitals and nursing homes, build retirement communities, finance civil rights workers, sponsor baseball games, and lend their organizers to work in community fund drives.

There are nearly 3,500 independent hospitals, and thousands more independent nursing homes. There are 1,357 private colleges and universities enrolling 1.7 million students, and more than 17,000 private schools. With the post-Sputnik demand for excellence, their enrollments now grow at a faster rate than public schools.

* The fraternal groups once provided recreation and association for new urbanites; today, with record memberships and treasuries, they are one of the independent institutional forms which needs to find a bold new function worthy of their resources.

More than two thousand United Funds and Community Chests collect and dispense nearly half a billion dollars a year.

More than that, there are 4,755,000 business firms, many of which take on public responsibilities that have nothing to do with their basic job of turning a profit. West Virginia Pulp and Paper spent $4.5 million to clean up the polluted north branch of the Potomac River. Corporate contributions to colleges, a relatively minor activity until the fifties, now increase by 15 per cent annually. Far larger is industry's annual investment of $4.5 billion or more in employee education. General Electric Company educates more people in New York State than any other institution, public or private. Business executives give time worth perhaps $5 billion a year to charitable causes, and many universities depend heavily on successful lawyers and other professionals for part-time teachers.

Had enough? These are tremendous raw resources. I can hardly imagine a task too great for them. And the potential of the independent sector has, if anything, grown faster than the commercial sector's strength. Our conquest of toil greatly multiplies the "leisure" time we can use for the public service that enriches private life. Economist Marion Clawson figures Americans will have 660 billion more hours of leisure in the year 2000 than we did in 1950.

If fully mobilized, the independent sector could, I believe:

(1) Put to work everyone who is willing and able to work.
(2) Wipe out poverty.
(3) Find and solve the farm problem.
(4) Give everyone good medical care.
(5) Stop juvenile crime.
(6) Renew our towns and cities, and turn anonymous slums into human communities.

(7) Pay reasonable retirement benefits to all.

(8) Replace hundreds of government regulations with more effective codes of conduct, vigorously enforced by each profession and an alert press.

(9) Handle the nation's total scientific research effort.

(10) Turn our foreign policy into a world crusade for human welfare and personal dignity.

(11) Lever a wider distribution of stock ownership.

(12) Stop air and water pollution.

(13) Give every person the education he needs, wants, and can profit by.

(14) Provide cultural and recreational outlets for everyone who wants them.

(15) Wipe out racial segregation.

The independent sector has the power to do these formidable things. But, curiously, as its strength has increased we have given it less and less to do, and assigned more and more common tasks to government. The next chapter explains why.

7

The Failure of
the Independent Sector

The independent sector often puts its resources to work magnificently. It is capable of stunning social accomplishments.

A national private organization, as we have seen, just about wiped out polio.

America's "worst" community, Chicago's back-of-the-yards, the setting for Upton Sinclair's *The Jungle,* long ago took its affairs into its own hands and renewed itself. Saul Alinsky, a leader with a gift for getting results, shaped the harsh drive toward clear goals. The people living back-of-the-yards faced problems that would send most communities screaming to Washington in despair—not enough jobs, slum housing, rats, racketeers, dope, illiteracy. But back-of-the-yards now wins awards because it is so clean and orderly. When a problem comes up, the people solve it. The meat packers who employed many of the people in back-of-the-yards are now moving out of Chicago. So the back-of-the-yards Neighborhood Council goes out and recruits new industry. Its main asset? Hard-working people you can count on. The Jungle has become a showcase of independent action. And Alinsky, his methods tested and proved, has turned to organizing the Negro drive to wipe out Chicago's South Side slum.

In Indianapolis, Cleo Blackburn set out to renew a Negro slum. He got the banks to lend money for land and materials. He copied the technical methods of Indiana's prefabricated housing industry—so he could use unskilled labor to build houses. He persuaded a foundation to pay the small cost of a technical center to coach the men on how to work. He organized the slum-dwellers into teams, and together they built their houses. The bank took their work as a down payment—sweat equity, Blackburn calls it. The people have built hundreds of houses this way. They've renewed the face and spirit of their community, which is now driving confidently into a total attack on hard-core unemployment.

On Long Island, an independent organization led by Henry Viscardi, a paraplegic, has helped hundreds of crippled people become completely self-supporting. He restores their spirit and determination, and then, often using specially designed equipment and machinery, offers them solid, soul-satisfying work to do.*

The Mormons take care of all the welfare needs of all members, and did so through the Depression.

Alcoholics Anonymous seldom fails to help an alcoholic who actually wants help.

Another independent organization, Recovery, Inc., now helps mental patients rebuild their lives by A.A.'s methods.

Charles Lavin has converted older luxury hotels into apartments and given older people comfortable room and board for as little as $86.50 a month. He made it possible for residents to pay part of this cost by helping with the work.

* An account of some of these people and their work can be found in Viscardi's *A Laughter in the Lonely Night* (Fawcett, 1963).

The independent Sears Foundation puts doctors in rural areas by showing communities exactly how they can attract and hold young doctors.

In 1955, a thirty-seven-year-old Presbyterian minister, Millard Roberts, took charge of Iowa's Parsons College. The college was dead on its feet: it owed its creditors $1.2 million; it had only 212 students. Its yearly income was $194,000; its deficit, $116,000. It valued its plant at $700,000. Faculty salaries averaged $2,800 a year. By 1963, Parsons had paid its long-term debt, its plant was worth $5 million; it had 2,200 students; faculty salaries averaged $13,000; its yearly income was $4,700,000. The percentage of faculty members with doctors degrees had increased from 23 to 80 per cent. While other college presidents were standing in line for federal money, Roberts arranged a $4.4 million loan from a bank at going rates to build an even bigger campus.

But the independent sector, in spite of its great strength and sporadically incredible achievements, is rapidly falling behind the burgeoning commercial and government sectors. It seems to be running out of things to do, and losing the gift for taking on new projects. More than 90 per cent of the money we spend for welfare now flows through government. We spend less than 10 per cent through the independent sector.

The independent sector once handled nearly all medical research. Some experts say government will finance 70 per cent of it by 1970. College education, once provided almost entirely by the independent sector, will be 70 per cent governmental by 1970. Experts, assuming little growth for independent colleges, predict that higher education will be 85 per cent governmental by 1985.

The federal government supports or controls two thirds of our scientific research and development effort.

The independent sector still serves important needs in recreation and culture. But the government is moving rapidly into these fields—often, as in Washington's Kennedy Center for the Performing Arts—with the help of independent funds.

What's the trouble? Why is the importance of this vast potential so rapidly declining? Why do we ignore this great and growing strength of the independent sector when we form public policy? Why does a leading economist contend that it is fit only to maintain dog cemeteries and sanctuaries for birds?

The answer is simple. The independent sector is now unreliable. It performs unevenly. Its brilliant achievements stand in contrast to miserable failures, to a stubborn backwardness.

I live in California, but my work often takes me to New York. Every so often, something like this happens: I leave New York at four in the afternoon in a jet that puts me in San Francisco at six-thirty. With luck, I can make a seven-o'clock board meeting of the local unit of a private welfare agency with which I've worked for several years. The contrast is incredible. My airline reservation has been handled by a computer; the plane crosses the continent in five hours, safely and comfortably. But at the board meeting I may hear a report on how many lap robes the needlework committee knitted and stitched together the month before. The airline, in the commercial sector, operates in the twentieth century and has made it the jet age. The welfare agency, in the independent sector, still operates in the nineteenth century, and is genially content with rustic methods.

The commercial sector has led the way into radically new technology, new markets, and new forms of organization. The government sector has, by a more recent surge, grown enormously in size and scope. It has even become the largest single customer for computers. But the independent sector did not keep the pace. It stumbled blindly into the twentieth century. It failed to grasp the new demands placed upon it and develop new methods to meet them.

We still roll bandages and knit mufflers in the missile age.

We preserve quaint vestiges of once practical ideas. Two hundred years ago, colleges closed down in the summer so the boys could help on the farm. Most colleges still do. In a farm economy where money was scarce, people staged bazaars and other money-making sociables to raise bits of cash for charity. Such events live on, quaint now in a money economy, as the fiscal backbone of many independent institutions.

Naturally the independent sector loses ground when it attempts to use cracker-barrel methods on space-age problems. It runs Scout troops and bird sanctuaries and campaigns against litter, but it is no longer considered able to take serious public responsibility. It does only the jobs nobody thinks are very important. The independent sector plays a large but shrinking role in America. It seems to be going out of style. We preserve many independent institutions in the same spirit San Francisco preserves a few cable cars—not because we really need them, but because they remind us of a part of our past that we know was good.

We assign less and less public business to the independent sector, not because we find it incapable—its great achievements belie that—but because it seems unreliable. You can assign an alcoholic reporter an occasional story, and he may perform brilliantly; but you can't put him on the city desk, where dereliction would mean disaster. We still give the independent sector occasional minor assignments where failure would be regrettable but not disastrous.

Can we rehabilitate the independent sector? Will it once again become a main contender for social responsibility in America? I believe it will, because we are beginning to understand why it didn't adjust to the new world we live in. And we are beginning, often by useful accidents, to see how it can.

8

What Took Us
So Long

In 1705, a Dutch-born philosopher named Bernard Mandeville published in England a satire called *Fable of the Bees*. This perverse little essay showed how evil men often contribute more to society than good men. Oddly enough, *Fable* proved to be one of history's really important works. It lighted the long fuse which in time detonated the Industrial Revolution.

Mandeville had stubbed his toe on a curious phenomenon. He saw that selfish personal behavior often led to good social results. "Private vices," he subtitled the book, "make public benefits." He contended that greed, an ultimate evil in the feudal world, often drove people to do things which brought benefits to others.

No one had really grasped this nettle before. The moral tradition of the time was built on what scholars call the Montaigne dogma, which says simply that the good things of this world are firmly fixed in quantity; hence, one man's gain must be another man's loss. You could only enrich yourself by impoverishing somebody else. So greed was antisocial, a sin against your fellow men.

Although he didn't know it at the time, Mandeville's satire

blew the Montaigne dogma forever out of the water. He had discovered that man's acquisitive impulse, in other words the profit motive, actually generates new wealth. If so, greed need not be morally suppressed. When held in check by competition, greed could serve the public good. Organizing commercial activity around the profit motive turned out, in time, to be the only really sensible way to conduct a nation's economic affairs. It put the vital force of each man's selfishness to work for society.

Mandeville merely stated the "private vices—public benefits" dilemma. It was left to Adam Smith to resolve it. In his monumental *Wealth of Nations,* he told the world clearly and comprehensively what made commerce work. There is an astonished tone in his work, as if he could hardly believe his own discoveries and sensed a quality of magic in them. He sorted out and explained in rich detail the basic forces which move and discipline commercial action. He spoke eloquently of the "invisible hand" which arranged economic resources in their most productive combinations.* Once men understood Smith's principle, they could deliberately shape public and private policy to work with the grain of economic principle rather than across it.

The result is history. Before Smith, commercial progress had been uneven and, in a sense, accidental. Isolated examples of sound commercial activity appeared whenever the power of the profit motive was inadvertently released. For example, the Jews, forced into commerce because smug Christians excluded them from almost everything else, became the accidental pioneers of free enterprise. Other gifted individuals here and there built useful enterprises. But the success of these isolated efforts could not become general until Smith identified, explained, and, in so doing,

---

* Smith's latter-day critics decided that the invisible hand was the hoof of the devil. His too-fervent disciples jumped to the conclusion that the invisible hand could do all of society's work. I think both groups are unjust to each other—and especially to Adam Smith.

legitimized the basic forces at work in the commercial sector.

At the intellectual level, scholars could now build a rich new body of theoretical and practical literature—the literature of political economy. At the practical level, the commercial sector began to spread itself, slowly at first and then, especially in America, at an ever accelerating rate. Enterprisers developed new methods of organizing commercial energy: the corporate form of organization at one level, assembly-line production at another. Accounting, the commercial sector's unique system of notation, grew more complex and sophisticated, and became the constant, precise monitor of efficiency. Now we could take the world's raw resources—human energy and physical materials (resources which had been there all the time)—and put them together into ever more fabulously productive combinations.

Today the independent sector stands about where the commercial sector stood in the centuries before we knew why it worked. Its performance is uneven because it works by accident. There are some brilliant individual operators —men like Henry Viscardi, Saul Alinsky, Cleo Blackburn, Tom Dooley (see Chapter 7)—but because we don't know why they succeed when others fail, we cannot put their work into general use.

Millard Roberts, who has succeeded so brilliantly at Parsons College, was a happy accident (see Chapter 7). He was, I suspect, sent to that broken-down college as a punishment for what his less aggressive superiors termed a lack of humility in his duties as a young clergyman. Some thought he could do little more than preside over the school's liquidation. Instead, he succeeded—partly because he is very able, partly because he is one of those people who temperamentally have to succeed, and partly because few vested interests were left at Parsons to stop him. He adapted the tested techniques of commerce to the work of Parsons College, setting out to do what every businessman has to do—to produce, as he says, "a better product for less money." He took the best that was known about how to run a college and systematically put this know-how to work: he simplified the curriculum, established a trimester system for full-time use of the plant, introduced team-teaching, priced his product realistically and built his new buildings economically. His trustees gave him unusual freedom because the college had nowhere to go but up.

Sadly, the efficiency of Parsons is a rare and accidental exception to the rule—not only in education, but throughout the independent sector.

Examples:

- A friend of mine studied the operation of a school for poor mountain boys. When he figured the cost per boy, he found it would have been cheaper to send them all to England's famous Eton School, and pay the travel cost.
- One family agency I know spends $18 to deliver an hour of family counseling. Another spends only $5.
- Studies by Sheldon and Eleanor Glueck and other experts show that conventional "character building" and recreation agencies have little effect on juvenile delinquency. Yet these agencies still use up a heavy and growing percentage of private welfare dollars.

The independent sector, then, uses men and material badly. It doesn't signal needs properly. It doesn't fill shortages automatically. Inefficiency is not punished by failure. We have, as yet, no way to figure out the independent sector's tasks and priorities. Its agencies penalize fraud, but not incompetence. The course offerings in one Southern college catalog outnumber its enrolled students. Most colleges use their monumental buildings only part-time. "I know many college campuses where a gunshot in the middle of the afternoon would not only hit no one; there would scarcely be anyone to hear it," said Dr. Harold Stokes when he was president of New York's Queens College.

If you ask an independent agency, "How much do you need?" it can only answer "More," and then spend the money carelessly. The equipment for open-heart surgery costs $100,000, and hospitals need ten skilled people to operate it. One Midwestern town fitted out six of its eight hospitals with this equipment, which was far more than was needed.

Such practices couldn't last in the commercial sector. But in the independent sector, we don't channel resources to those who use them well or away from those who use them carelessly. Independent effort has only an accidental relationship to real "demand" and efficient "production." Thus, the independent sector often spends its money and energy blindly. It has a large, but always limited, amount of money and energy to spend. It doesn't know how to ration it. It doesn't know when to start spending money or when to stop. It doesn't know how to adapt itself to shifting needs. It doesn't know how to copy good practices or how best to devise new ones.

How do we know, for example, when to stop spending money on hospitals and start spending it for job training? How should we divide money between basic and applied research? How much should we spend for research on heart disease? How much on cancer? How much should we spend for nursing homes? How much for Scout camps? How much for scholarships? How much for college buildings?

The independent sector doesn't know and currently seems to have no way to find out. So, inevitably, we invest resources in weird ways. You may have noticed specific cases:

- Study after study shows that 20 per cent of the people in hospitals needn't be there. Several years ago, a medical audit of California revealed that there were twice as many hospital beds as the population needed, but in some parts of the state there were not nearly enough.

• *Look* magazine found "more facilities for training and supplying seeing-eye dogs than there are blind people who want them." Retarded children outnumber cerebral palsy victims ten to one, but the latter get four times as much money. And *Look* continued: "The help given 250,000 multiple-sclerosis cases was about equal to that given 11 million sufferers from arthritis and rheumatism."

The independent sector seems to drift, moving blindly and without discipline. Its power lies raw and undeveloped. It often seems listless, sluggish, passive, and defensive. The commercial and government sectors have outrun it. Who can blame people for thinking they are the only sectors to count on for serious responsibility in modern America?

But I believe a radical change is close upon us. We saw, in the first third of this century, a productive explosion of America's commercial sector and, simultaneously, a growing recognition of its limitations. In the second third we've seen an immensely educational experiment with big government and a growing realism about its limitations, its costs in wasted resources and human dignity. In the last third of the twentieth century, the immense idle capacity of our independent sector will, I believe, unfold in ways that will astonish us all. Why? Because, for the first time, we are beginning to understand the basic forces at work in the independent sector. We are coming to know why and how independent action works. And as we do, we will find ways to harness these natural resources and multiply the output of independent energy.

What took us so long? Only now are many people groping to understand independent action.* The reason may be

---

* In my own work I have been astonished at how many other people are earnestly exploring the same unmapped region. I feel like someone

simple: we were never forced to understand it before. In a cracker-barrel society, before our era of mass organization, people took practical independent action whether they understood it or not. They knew each other, as conservative writer Frank Meyer points out, and thus felt the imperative to help each other. The instruments in a simple society were more obvious. But now we have to identify the forces at work in the independent sector before we can organize to work in the modern world.

Everything that moves with a purpose needs two forces —a driving power and a directing system. The wind in a boat's sail makes it go. But it would waver aimlessly without a rudder, which restrains and directs it.

As we have seen, Smith identified the two forces at work in commercial action. The pursuit of profit drives the commercial sector. Competition directs it, disciplines its effort. Henry Ford II is no philosopher but he knows what makes business tick: "[The profit system] works because it harnesses human drives to constructive purposes . . . it provides incentives that stimulate masses of people in a constant restless search for greater efficiency." Survival and profit depend on figuring out tomorrow's needs and organizing to meet them. But the competitive system goes beyond moving men to act; it shows them where and how. Business is efficient, not because it wants to be or because a special breed of people run it, but because it has to be— because competition makes it use resources efficiently. If a business loses control of its costs, it sinks into a competitive sea. If it loses touch with what its customers need and want, it sinks. Businesses prosper when they give customers better service for less money. Those which don't, fail. Capital flows in to expand those which use it well; capital shrinks from those which use it badly. The system works automatically; nobody steers it from headquarters.

---

who struggled to climb the highest mountain, and, arriving, blundered into a Sunday school picnic.

Though not always perfect, it works as if Smith's invisible hand were always at the tiller. Competition continuously redirects the energy our pursuit of profit generates.

We find two analogous forces in the independent sector —a powerful driving force and a stern directing force. The next two chapters discuss them in turn.

9

The Independent Sector's Driving Force

---※---

Independent institutions, when compared with commerce and government, seem at first glance not to have any powerful driving force. The other two sectors have obvious energy sources. In the commercial sector, the motivation is the desire for profit. In the government sector, the motivation is the desire for power. Both motives, shaped by specialized institutions, drive men and women to strong, persistent effort. One produces material wealth beyond all belief; the other produces, indeed overproduces, the welfare state. But in the independent sector, the motivation, in its purest form, is the desire to serve others. Unless this drive is stronger than many people now assume or is reinforced by other motives, the third sector is like a giant truck with a toy engine.

Is it? The cynic about human nature insists that men, like mules, will act only to get to the carrot (profit) or to avoid the stick (government coercion). This stripped-down concept of mankind supports the popular notion that American life has only two major sectors, one based on profit and one on power. If so, politics can never be more than a bitter struggle between business and bureaucracy. We have built-in class warfare.

It has nevertheless become the intellectual fashion, and a mark of sophistication, to deny that any selfless motive exists in people. Often the very men who dedicate their lives to serving others explain human action in terms of this stylish cynicism. My friend Saul Alinsky, whose superb work in our distressed communities was mentioned briefly in Chapter 7, absolutely rejects the service motive. He believes there is no interest beyond self-interest. Saul works among very poor people, organizing power centers to put force behind their demands for fair play, and hotly rejects as naïve and sentimental the idea that any community will ever voluntarily offer equal opportunities to minorities caught in the cruel machinery of modern society. The profit motive he recognizes. The power motive he glorifies. The service motive? It would be nice if people had it, but they don't, so forget it. The catch is that Saul's dogma doesn't explain his dedication.

A few intellectual pioneers, however, have begun to break down this barrier, and come to a more realistic view of what men are like. The change can be found all along the political spectrum. Harvard's David Riesman, author of *The Lonely Crowd* and a bomb-banning liberal, treats the tough-minded people-are-no-damn-good cult as a new form of hyprocrisy. "In Victorian days, the hypocrite was a man who pretended to be better than he was," Reisman told a student last year. "In the post-Freudian era, a hypocrite is apt to be a man who pretends to be *worse* than he is. This is equally misleading. I am not sure but what the Victorian hypocrisy was more useful, for the talk held out the prospect of getting better, while post-Freudian hypocrisy encourages us to be worse."

So the course of modern thought has begun to turn. There is growing dissatisfaction with the wiseacre view that man is only a pig on two legs. In theology, in literature, even in gay Broadway plays like *The Music Man,* we see an all-out search for deeper human meaning, for human action beyond egotism.

But meanwhile, the "existentialists" of modern thought have given us something deeply important, often without knowing just what they did. They've shown us vividly that if human life is only a bundle of selfish, mechanical impulses, then life isn't worth the trouble. On this premise, life is indeed absurd, as one despairing cult of existentialists insist. Rollo May, an existential psychoanalyst, points to the apathy in modern America. What causes it? Says May: "[People] who treat themselves as machines are less and less able to feel toward themselves and other people."

Editors set up committees to hunt for a national purpose. Here, for all to see, is a shocking declaration of moral bankruptcy, the loss of the satisfaction we once got from personal purpose and action. "The clamorous search for national goals," says University of Michigan philosopher Abraham Kaplan (*Saturday Review,* December 23, 1961), "does not stem from democracy's loss of purpose but from our loss of faith in its citizens. We are characters in search of an author, while the greatness of the drama lies in just this: that the characters themselves take over the plot."

The characters have now begun to take over in unexpected ways. The liberal press has been dumfounded by the power of the conservative movement among young people and among responsible community leaders. Though the protest has lacked a program and occasionally turns silly, conservatives are making liberal reporters understand that they do not represent reaction. They seem to be engaged, wrote a puzzled columnist, in a new moral crusade. Conservative writer Alice Widener got closer to the point with an article on "Babbitt's Revolt." Businessmen and others, she said, who know they want to serve their communities, are rebelling against the stale charge that they are all self-serving squares.

I believe one of the most significant events of 1965 came in March, when a thousand Peace Corps veterans gathered in Washington to talk about what to do now that they have returned to private life. Here was a special group. Some had, of course, joined the Peace Corps for kicks, or to defer a tough career decision, or to escape final exams. But the impulse the Corps set out to organize was the individual's desire to serve. It was a government organization, but the volunteers in their daily work overseas often acted more like organizers of independent action than like government agents. (In India, they even started a co-op chicken industry.) Coming back this year, having tasted the satisfaction of personal service, the veterans were grimly determined to find permanent ways to "make a difference" as individuals, at home or abroad.

The Peace Corps veterans astonished the older people at their convention. More than ever burning with idealism, they wouldn't buy the easy-sounding solutions that used to satisfy "socially conscious" young people. After three days of constant workshops, they did not recommend a single new federal program. Instead, the overwhelming majority insisted again and again that each of them had to find his own chance for direct service. They were impatient with any bureaucratic rules or barriers that got in the way of the opportunity to serve. Some put their new beliefs into political language. Jerome Reinish, who served in Venezuela, got a nervous laugh with this remark: "I went to City College as a Socialist and graduated a Democrat, and I think the Peace Corps has nearly made me a Republican." His point wasn't political. He meant simply that like many other corpsmen, he had developed a healthy suspicion of bureacracy and had found an intense joy in "personal involvement."

The newspapers kept reporting (to the anger of the Corps veterans) that the group seemed "frustrated," but they missed the nature of the frustration. The vets agreed, as one speaker put it, that "the country doesn't owe you a cause." But how, in modern America, do you find your own? This was the root of their frustration as they talked for three days. These earnest young people were finding that American institutions now offer all too few opportunities for direct, important service to a cause. They felt very much like a similar number of Young Republicans I had met a few weeks earlier at a training school in Washington. In different political language, both conventions of young people were searching for the "chance to make a difference." They are, I believe, moving instinctively to revive the independent sector. And when they see hope conceptualized in the independent sector idea, they don't let you go to bed before dawn.

This drying up of opportunities for personal service has been urgent for some time. Four or five years ago, when I first began to sense the importance of this gap, I began to watch the papers for illustrations of the service motive at work in America. What struck me, as my files filled up with examples, was not that people acted, but that they often overacted on the rare occasions when they could see both a specific human need and a way to do something about it.

The following summaries of press reports illustrate the frustration that sometimes leads to bizarre overaction once a need becomes obvious, and gets in the papers.

In 1959, on a cold, rainy December night, a helicopter crashed in the Potomac River. Ten critically injured people were taken to a local hospital. A radio station broadcast an appeal for blood at midnight. The *Washington Evening Star* reported:

Hundreds of would-be donors converged on the institution. The response caused a traffic jam that took half a dozen policemen to straighten out.

Many parked their cars three blocks away and walked through the rain. One couple arrived carrying a baby, and a man who heard the broadcast on his radio pulled up beside a police patrol car on the outskirts of Leesburg, Virginia, and asked to be escorted to the hospital.

Several donors appeared wearing their overcoats over pajamas. Hospital officials estimated, at one time, more than 200 persons were in the lobby or outside standing in the rain waiting to donate.

A little Negro girl in our county wrote a letter to the paper, addressing the thief of a bicycle she had saved for months to buy. The thief didn't respond. But thirty-five people offered her another bike.

When tiny Doreen Heskitt disappeared from her home in Napa, California, five thousand people went to help find her.*

Albert Schweitzer is another significant symbol. Why has he become a household word? His outdated medical technique shocks doctors who visit his Lambaréné mission. His patronizing attitude toward Africans outrages the proud new nationalist leaders. Yet his name strikes a lost chord in the soul of modern men and women. A brilliant scholar and musician as a young man, he had the world at his feet, but he made a dramatic decision to lose himself in service to black people nobody else cared about. He has been sainted by millions, I believe, because his life is so full of what they most urgently want.

* If these examples demonstrate an unrequited lust to serve, they also reveal a failure of the press. Because reporters accept the popular premise that only government and business carry on the serious business of the society, they tend to report independent action only when it is quaint or sentimental. Few see that the independent sector even now carries on a major part of the nation's public business, and that it can do much more.

Schweitzer saw what was missing from the two-sector society. "I am convinced," he once said, "that there is far more . . . of idealist will-power than ever comes to the surface of the world . . . the idealism which becomes visible is small in proportion to what men and women bear locked in their hearts, unreleased or scarcely released." The irony of Schweitzer's life is that, by self-denial, he partly monopolized something other men desperately needed. This year, in an interview with *Life,* he offered to lend his discovery to others. "Everyone," he said, "can have his own little Lambaréné."

Whether the desire to serve arises from self-denial or egomania, it is a compelling drive. If you look honestly about you, forgetting your schoolbook psychology, you may come to share my belief that the service motive is at least as powerful as the desire for profit or power. We see some people in whom it is paramount and overwhelming, just as some men seem to have no other interest than the stubborn pursuit of wealth or power. But we see the service motive to some degree in almost everyone.

We naturally see the service motive in many alloys, since human motives are always mixed. Charitable contributions are tax-deductible; the deduction invites more people to give more, and fortifies the service motive. A public benefactor may get his name in the paper and like it. This strengthens, rather than weakens, the machinery of the independent sector. If the National Association of Manufacturers can help business wipe out unemployment, rather than pay higher taxes for doubtful expansion of federal efforts, then the profit motive stimulates independent action. And if the desire for political power inspires politicians to work in the independent sector to earn respect and votes, the independent sector gains added strength.

Those who deny the existence of the desire to serve see mounting human problems and few people doing anything. They read of a girl who dies screaming in a New York street, her murder coolly witnessed by a dozen bystanders who made no move to help. They see the distress of migrant workers, Negroes, slum-dwellers, the mentally ill. The very existence of these problems in an affluent society screams "Who Cares?" But inaction doesn't mean people don't care. It means, I believe, that people want to help, but don't know how to put their concern to work.

Consider the examples listed earlier in this chapter. In each case, the need was obvious and the way individuals could be helpful was very clear. When Doreen Heskitt got lost in Napa, her problem was obvious: she couldn't find her way home. It was equally clear what a concerned individual could do: go to Napa and help look for her. Blood donations are the classic example. People are offered a very specific way to help fellow men in distress, and they line up to do it.

The service motive seems weak only because we have failed to find ways to apply it to complex modern problems. We see it at work only in simple, nineteenth-century ways. And this contributes to the illusion that the independent sector is unfit for modern responsibility.*

New vision in developing personal outlets for the service motive is desperately needed. Their decline sharply constricts the scope of the human enterprise. A man who only works and votes and pays his taxes is scarcely a whole man. "Reverence for life," says Dr. Schweitzer in his persistent way, "demands from all that they should sacrifice a portion of their own lives for others." But now, increasingly, we can only help our fellow man through middlemen, through remote political institutions. Lacking a direct outlet for our hunger to help others, to add the full dimension of meaning to our lives, we are frustrated and incomplete.

* But in the feudal world, the profit motive must have appeared weak or nonexistent. Primitive cottage industry was then its largest achievement. Commercial productivity exploded only when a favorable climate forced men to develop modern methods of organization.

The consequences may be worse than we think. Alexis de Tocqueville, who identified the independent sector as our finest tradition (Chapter 5), also saw that without it our society would in time become barbaric. "A people," Tocqueville wrote in *Democracy in America*, "among whom individuals lost the power of achieving great things single-handed, without acquiring the means of producing them by united exertions, would soon relapse into barbarism" (Volume II, Second Book, Chapter V). Does the rise of irresponsibility and crime in the U.S. mean this grim prediction is coming true?

Tocqueville put his warning into political prophecy: "It is vain to summon a people, which has been rendered so dependent on a central power, to choose from time to time the representatives of that power; this rare and brief exercise of their free choice, however important it may be, will not prevent them from gradually losing the faculties of thinking, feeling and acting for themselves, and thus gradually falling below the level of humanity" (Volume II, Fourth Book, Chapter V). This is the final danger of an ever expanding welfare state.

Tocqueville did not foresee a cold war on this small planet. He did not know how quickly an internal weakness might become a daily threat to survival. But his analysis can be applied to the world situation. Not long ago I was discussing the potential of the independent sector with one of our chief civilian defense strategists, and was startled at the eagerness of his reaction. I asked him about it. "You see," he said, "we do not know how to defend a passive people. Unless we overcome people's growing diffidence, we have no effective strategy."

We are a nation of people with great ability and incredible power. But we have so limited our chances for personal action that we can only lament the spirit we have lost and wonder why we were put here with so little to do. The demand of the future is to release the idealistic will power, as Schweitzer called it, that has been bottled up with such alarming human consequences. We need first of all to identify the force which can give direction to the untapped power of the service motive.

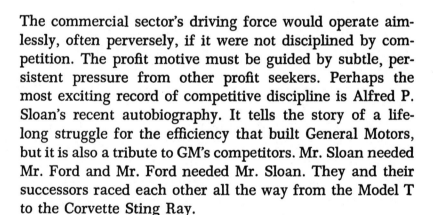

10

The Independent Sector's Discipline

The commercial sector's driving force would operate aimlessly, often perversely, if it were not disciplined by competition. The profit motive must be guided by subtle, persistent pressure from other profit seekers. Perhaps the most exciting record of competitive discipline is Alfred P. Sloan's recent autobiography. It tells the story of a lifelong struggle for the efficiency that built General Motors, but it is also a tribute to GM's competitors. Mr. Sloan needed Mr. Ford and Mr. Ford needed Mr. Sloan. They and their successors raced each other all the way from the Model T to the Corvette Sting Ray.

In contrast, the independent sector lives in the horse-and-buggy days. It seems quaint, old-fashioned, unsuited for the jet pace of modern life. The press, as noted in the previous chapter, does a cute little story on it once in a while. Our failure to recognize and harness the service motive is one reason for the sector's low state. The other reason for the independent sector's backwardness is our failure to understand what disciplines and channels independent action. This chapter describes the disciplining force.

The independent sector has a natural competitor: government. Both sectors operate in the same industry: public service and welfare. Sometimes, over the years, leaders on each side have sensed their competitive positions and built a fascinating record of both creative competition and deliberate collusion. The quality of life in the U. S. now depends largely on the revival of a lively competition between these two natural contenders for public responsibility. The struggle would enhance the effectiveness of both.

The weak sister is the independent sector. With the raw resources to make a lively bid (Chapter 6), it fails to put its competitive potential to work. The very idea of competition with government is, by a weird public myth, thought to be illegitimate, disruptive, divisive, unproductive, and perhaps immoral.* The result is roughly analogous to what would have happened had Mr. Ford decided one day that it would be more gentlemanly to build just a few cars for his friends and encourage Mr. Sloan, unchallenged by Ford's genius, to go after the big market. The market in cars, like today's market in public services, would have offered a poorer product, less choice.

The idea that competition with government is pernicious came along fairly recently. Just fifty years ago, the Rockefeller Foundation and the Carnegie Corporation together spent twice as much for education and social service as did the entire federal government. Voluntary agencies took the lion's share of public responsibility. The issue of the day was the reverse of the present: Should the government dare compete with the big boys in the independent sector? In 1915, the Walsh Commission on Industrial Relations (created by Congress in 1912) issued an historic, if now forgotten, report involving American philanthropy.†

* In much the same way, the commercial sector's competitive concept was suppressed for centuries as a source of social disorder.

† The Commission's report touched on philanthropy because the notorious Ludlow massacre occurred at a Rockefeller-controlled mining location.

Though the majority voted for a monopoly in welfare service (then held by private agencies), two commissioners wrote a truculent dissent on behalf of aggressive government:

> There should be no alliance between . . . private foundations . . . and the government . . . the state should use its money to displace [private charity] by better and more universal charity. Instead of calling upon private foundations for help, the Government should treat them as competitors.

In the years that followed, government pressed persistently for responsibility. For a time, government's relationship to the independent sector was overtly competitive, and leaders in the independent sector recognized it. As late as 1931, the Red Cross turned down a proposed Congressional grant of $25 million to help drought sufferers; instead they tried to raise $10 million to do the job alone. "All we pray for is that you [Congress] let us alone and let us do the job," said the chairman of the Red Cross central committee.

Then, as the Depression demolished public confidence in independent action, government assumed vast new responsibilities. Independent institutions tried heroically to meet the mounting problems which suddenly poured in on them, but the public considered their efforts inadequate and supported with little reservation government-offered solutions.

Even as the Depression gave way to the mobilization boom and then to an unheard-of postwar prosperity, government kept up its steady pressure for more and more responsibility.* The independent sector, its confidence badly

---

* We persist in saying that when a public problem develops, "the government is forced to step in," implying that government doesn't ever want to act; that it acts reluctantly. This, of course, is perfect nonsense. In his 1962 annual report, the Secretary of Health, Education and Welfare, wrote:

We are not content with our national posture in education. . . . We

shaken, overwhelmed by the booming growth of its government competitor, never recovered its capacity to take a big share of social responsibility. By 1961, an *ad hoc* commission on voluntary welfare agencies, financed by the Rockefeller Foundation and manned mostly by captains of industry, wrote the new case for a public service cartel —this time with the independent agencies reduced to limited subsidiaries of government:

> It is important for voluntary agencies to recognize that they are allies, not competitors [with government], in providing . . . health and welfare services. It is important . . . that voluntary agencies not be used as a means to oppose the development of government services.

In short, the 1961 Commission believed that the independent sector, which government competition had almost pushed off the board, should not compete—should do nothing but get out of the way. So, in fifty years since the Walsh Commission, the picture had been exactly reversed. It had been thought improper for government to compete with independent institutions. Now it is considered improper for independent institutions to compete with government.

We have gone even further. Many believe that the independent sector's main function is to assist the government in its effort to take more responsibility, often by providing pilot projects and press agentry. Most of our great national health and welfare groups have registered as Washington lobbyists, and they argue consistently for bigger govern-

---

will continue to press for measures to strengthen our schools and colleges.
And later:
It is not possible in this fast-moving age to stop and say we are done. We can only pause from time to time and say we have begun—knowing that other beginnings, other tasks, await our attention tomorrow.
This is scarcely the language of a reluctant contender for social responsibility.

ment. "Sensitive to the needs of people, volunteers have usually pushed for expanded government welfare programs," writes social work's Professor Charles N. Lebeaux in *The Citizen Volunteer* (Harper & Row, 1960).

When independent organizations collect money, they say it goes to cut down the need for tax-supported services. Then they use the money to lobby for more tax-supported services. Few leaders ever consider the duplicity of their action. For example, in the last few years colleges and universities have gone successfully after corporate dollars. The fund-raisers tell corporations these dollars will make federal aid unnecessary, yet, as the U. S. Commissioner of Education reports, "the virtually unanimous councils of higher education" say they must have federal aid.

A University of California researcher questioned board and staff members of a large number of private agencies. His unpublished study showed that 85 per cent of the board members and 90 per cent of the staff members wanted federal aid for mental health. And the independent National Association for Mental Health takes credit in its annual reports for "historic" increases in federal aid to mental health.

A distinguished consultant group on nursing says: "If the nursing problem is to be solved, there is no alternative to federal aid."

Most big private foundations think their main job is to show where we need more government action.

"Our leading private social agencies are asking . . . for strengthened public services," says the *Social Service Review*.

"Not the least of the accomplishments of the voluntary agencies," says *Science* magazine, "is the part they have played in persuading Congress to establish NIH [National Institutes of Health]."

"Major Gains Won in Congress," reads the headline of a paper published by the private National Association for

Retarded Children. What gains? More federal responsibility for retarded children.

The National Tuberculosis Association policy: "Support of legislative proposals and appropriations to make permanent those services necessary to the communities' tuberculosis and related health needs." Representatives meet "several times a year" with government "to discuss . . . existing programs, future program needs, and the financial appropriations necessary."

Ladies in the District of Columbia began a few years ago to serve hot lunches to 270 needy students. They soon quit. They gaily said they just wanted to show the value of the program so that tax-supported agencies would take it over for the long run.

"The voluntary or private social agencies," writes Dean Benjamin Youngdahl of the George Warren Brown School of Social Work, "can provide leadership in new fields, in experimentation and research, in giving support to sound public programs and in filling gaps here and there until the public is ready to accept the needed services."

The Family Service Association of America officially reports: "Demonstrations by private agencies must often precede government acceptance of a particular responsibility."

Thus the independent sector now mainly promotes its government competitor. The test of a good citizen is not that he takes responsibility, but that he successfully sends it to Washington. Community "leaders" organize people to help the federal executive agencies satisfy their natural appetite for responsibility.*

Some independent leaders don't go so far. They want to stay in business, but only as a yardstick. They think a near-monopoly of the public business by government is bound to come, so the independent sector should focus its energy

* Maybe this is leadership, or maybe it is what soldiers call an advance to the rear.

in a narrow corner. We should build an island of independent activity in the sea of government action. Then we'll have a standard against which we can test the efficiency of government from time to time. For example, one great foundation is spending a lot of its money to make a few of our strongest private colleges even stronger, in somewhat the same spirit in which Noah built the Ark. Except, of course, they don't expect the waters to recede.

Supporters of the "yardstick" principle at least see that someone must compete with government. But they are naïve to think that a passive competitor, living on a protected reservation like a buffalo, can long be much more than an oddity. You have heard the story about the minister who put a lion and a lamb together in an enclosure in front of his church to illustrate the power of love. Some of his colleagues, facing dwindling congregations, suspiciously asked how he managed his crowd-drawing stunt. He was affronted. It was a perfectly honest demonstration, he said. "All you have to do is replace the lamb from time to time." Similarly, a reluctant competitor for public responsibility can't live very long with a determined one. The yardstick principle rests on an attitude of resignation to defeat.

This accidental perversion of the independent sector's competitive role has far-reaching consequences. For, far from being illegitimate, lively competition with government is essential if our democratic institutions are to work sensibly. We have in Congress specific machinery for choosing the most serviceable competitor for a public chore.

On April 3, 1944, Washington correspondent Allen Drury, author of *Advise and Consent*, wrote in his personal journal:

Taft was in, thoughtfully clipping his fingernails with a small pair of scissors as he slowly considered the legislative problem. "Obviously something should be done," he said in that flat, reasonable voice, "but I hardly hold with the theory that Congress ought to be turned into an executive agency. Congress is a jury, in a sense, expressing the will of the people and passing on proposals put before it."

But as things now stand, the jury hears only one side of each case. One day in Washington several years ago, I arrived at the Senate Office Building about an hour early for an appointment. To kill time, I wandered into a Senate hearing room where a subcommittee was considering a bill to give the states some federal money to put libraries in remote areas. The chairman had just opened the hearing. It fascinated me. I came back after my conference and stayed right through. The by-play was entertaining. The Senators made little speeches along the way, beginning with remarks like, "I have always been a friend of books." One Senator rushed in to tell a testifying voter from his district, "Sorry just to have missed some of your excellent testimony," when he had obviously missed all of it.

The witnesses presented their facts carefully, if not engagingly. But as the day wore on, I began to realize that all the testimony favored the bill. All of it. The hearing continued the next day. All the witnesses backed the bill. They were sellers of books or bookshelves or people who worked in libraries. The hearing drew to a close. I thought it would end with no one speaking against the bill. But as the chairman raised his gavel, an aide pushed a paper over to him. "Oh, yes," he said, "I nearly forgot. We have the usual letter of objection from the Chamber of Commerce." The hearing was over.

Thinking I had stumbled onto an unusual case, I began to study Congressional hearings. On the average, 95 per cent of all testimony supports the growth of government. Very often, 100 per cent of the testimony supports what the executive branch proposes, or wants even more. The tiny minority rarely offers any choice, and its spokesmen only deny the need for what has been proposed or make canned speeches denouncing federal spending.

In hearings in 1959 on a law to start a federal program to relieve "distressed areas," the Senate heard 59 witnesses: 56 supported the bill; 3 opposed it. In hearings on the same kind of legislation in 1957, 110 witnesses appeared: 104 supported the federal program; 6 opposed it. The year before, the Senate committee heard 193 witnesses: 190 supported the program; 2 opposed it; one was neutral. The House heard 44: 43 supported the program, one opposed it.

This one-sided system of gathering evidence might be all right if Americans had some sure way to decide what government should and should not do. But we have no such demarcation line in our political thought; we never have had one. We have preferences, but no stubborn prejudices. We are a pragmatic people. We would rather get things done without government, but we often compromise. Some people preach ideology at us, but few voters are moved by these arguments: abstractions make us uncomfortable.

No one thinks that government has somehow been divinely ordained to deliver the mail. It is a practical matter. They know we need mail service. They don't think commercial mail service would work. They would, I feel sure, want to break up the Post Office if technology could provide a substitute for mail, or if they found that private enterprise could do the job better.*

On the other hand, Americans don't believe that private enterprise has been divinely ordained to deliver the milk. If private milk delivery broke down, they would, I feel sure, turn the job over to the government, Adam Smith and the Dairymen's Association notwithstanding. "I don't care

* In fact, the greater efficiency of the telephone and telegraph companies, as well as United Parcel Service, now cuts into the former Post Office monopoly over communication.

about philosophy," says one Congressman; "I do care about sewage treatment." And liberal Senator Frank Church wrote in *U.S. News & World Report* on May 6, 1963:

> The federal government has grown bigger, not because anyone planned it that way, not in pursuit of any conspiracy to concentrate power on the Potomac, not, indeed, because any body of doctrine required it, but simply because as the country grew and changed, problems arose which existing machinery could not solve, and new ways were worked out, usually on a trial-and-error basis, to meet them.
>
> What I am saying is that we have not been doctrinaire, holding something to be good or bad as soon as some label could be affixed to it, but pragmatic, looking for the solution most apt to work, whatever it might be.

In his ice-breaking 1962 Yale speech calling for new imagination on public policy, President Kennedy said, "Each case—science, urban renewal, education, agriculture, natural resources—must be determined on its own merits if we are to profit from our unrivaled ability to combine the strength of public and private agencies."

So the political leadership, without any strict doctrine to guide it, looks at only what will work and what won't when it rations public responsibility. This was fine when the independent sector offered them a choice, but since it quit competing, they have none. They have been reduced to critics and advocates of a giant public service monopoly.*

As society grows more complex, the public business becomes harder to understand. It's harder for the average man to know what it is. Technicalities hide it even from Congressmen, yet Congress, in shaping public policy on a problem, should know:

---

* President Kennedy, talking privately to California's Democratic boss Jesse "Big Daddy" Unruh, said just before his death that he did not blame people for fearing gigantic government (*Look*, November 17, 1964).

How many people are in trouble?
Why?
What are we already doing about it in all three sectors?
What else should we be doing?
Who should do it?

The questions seem simple enough, but the answers in a complex society can be fantastically complicated. Congress must get facts and find out what they mean.

Without an independent sector competing actively for public responsibility, Congressmen can look only to the federal bureaucracy for figures and their meaning. They have to base their arguments and votes on information worked up by a single competitor for public responsibility. We're a nation of people who wouldn't paint the back porch without getting competitive bids. But we build national policy on the claims of a lone contender for public responsibility.

The spokesman for federal action can't be "objective," any more than a General Motors salesman can be counted on to tell you what's wrong with a Chevrolet. Several years ago, a federal employee testified at a hearing to decide whether Congress should broaden a certain federal health program. Toward the end a Congressman asked him if he would speak on the other side of the question. The question puzzled the witness. He didn't understand. "I don't know what you mean by the other side," he said.

We cannot write public policy that makes sense unless more than one sector makes a bid for public responsibility in every suitable area. We build policy on grotesque evidence. We act sensibly only by chance. "It is a remarkable and depressing fact," says University of Chicago economist George Stigler, past president of the American Economic Association, "that the vast expansion of the economic activities of the state have not been based on rational analysis." There is no competition to force proponents of programs to establish a rational case.

We can't base policy on what a single interested contender claims is true. Policies set in a climate of statistical crisis are bound to be misshapen. We lose touch with reality. Late in 1963, *Life* published one of the many scary reports on automation's job-kill. By 1968, the writer worried, quoting an anonymous Labor Department expert, some 14.6 million workers may be crying for work. Since government was then the only serious bidder for a chance to attack the problem, the government was the authority *Life* listened to, even though the data soon proved to be silly.

Representative government doesn't mean much if the people we elect to Congress have no real choice. If you control any legislative body's data and options, you control its action. You may not get everything you want, but you won't get anything you don't. As Senator Taft said, "Congress is a jury acting on proposals laid before it." But the only proposals now laid before it are worked up by the federal executive.

"Nearly all of the headline-catching legislation in Congress now originates in the executive branch," says the *Wall Street Journal*. More and more, Congressmen only originate such bills as those naming cruisers, making snow shoveling compulsory in the District of Columbia, forbidding the use of stop watches in the Post Office, and proposing to ennoble the corn tassel as the national flower.

Already we hear a chorus of despair from Congress. The Brookings Institution recently held several off-the-record round tables, in which outstanding Congressmen of both parties took part. Among their candid comments:

"It is virtually impossible for the ordinary member [of Congress] to have any idea of what is going on."

"The terrifying thing is that we are talking about

the ability of Congress to make decisions on the basis of information furnished by the executive. . . ."

"We have to take things pretty much on faith."

"It is very difficult for a Congressman to know what the truth is or where to find it."

"I often have a hard time finding out what the issue is."

"You can't get facts now."

"Unless the administration volunteers the information, Congress is generally pretty helpless."

"Time after time we go on the floor not knowing anything about the subjects to be discussed."

"We are supposed to know all about domestic activities—about education, water pollution, small business problems, dams, etc. No matter how hard-working . . . a Congressman is . . . he just can't master these problems."

We could build sound policy if two equally determined contenders for public responsibility debated the facts down to the core and argued out alternative tactics. Congress could sort out conflicting claims as to what we needed to do and how best to do it. But without creative conflict, Congress loses control.* Either house may change politically from time to time as people react to the cost of big government, but party balance only affects the rate at which the executive expands.

Congress generally acts, sooner or later, on what the federal executive proposes. Medicare is an example: it lost after President Truman first proposed it in 1948, but the idea didn't die. The executive decides what we shall do; the politicians decide when we shall do it. The executive sets policies; Congress can decide only when it will adopt

* We seem to judge Congress on how many laws it passes. When the executive has all the initiative, a "good" Congress is simply one that approves its program. A Congress that resists is a "do-nothing" Congress. If we judged our courts the same way, an ambitious judge would notch his bench for every hanging.

them. Congress doesn't control the Administration; the Administration calls the tune in Congress. Parliamentary control, as Britain's Sydney and Beatrice Webb once wrote, becomes an "illusion and a sham." Congress mainly figures out how to pay for government in a way taxpayers will tolerate.

So government grows immune to popular control. We're reversing public opinion's historic role. Federal programs aren't developed to provide what people want. People are sold on supporting the executive product. The executive advertises directly to the public in the press to create demand for government action, and the reporters, concentrated in Washington, assume that no government action means no action at all. The Opinion Research Corporation says: "U.S. citizens can be led to embrace the welfare state, but they don't demand it." So long as people don't violently object to a specific, the executive goes implacably on. For example:

- Seventy-five per cent of the people want tighter relief rules, but the government is loosening the rules we have.
- Fifty per cent want less government lending to business, but government is increasing its loans to business.
- People would prefer, eight to one, to see privately owned rather than federally owned public utilities grow, but federal power generators proliferate like rabbits.
- In a recent survey, only 7 per cent of the people thought the arts needed government help. Only 2 per cent wanted government to act. Shortly after that, the Senate passed a bill initiating federal support for the arts.
- People prefer "private sector" action to federal action on juvenile delinquency, three to one; on job retraining two to one; on youth fitness three to one; yet the federal government is expanding rapidly in all these fields.
- Only 36 per cent of the people think the farm income

problem is "urgent," yet we spend over $6,000,000,000 annually for farm subsidies.

The government doesn't ignore public opinion because the people who run it are naturally perverse. It isn't wasteful because it is manned by wasteful people. C. Northcote Parkinson's wry books on bureaucracy don't indict people; they describe life in any monopoly. Without competition, the bureaucracy can't make government efficient or even sensibly decide what it needs to do. Nor can the situation be magically improved. We know from experience that no unitary social institution can reform itself. Innovation painfully disrupts its way of life. Reform comes only through competitive outsiders who force steady, efficient adjustment to changing situations.

Independent sector leaders genially speak of complementing government, not competing with it—as if monopoly were good and competition destructive—thus unwittingly conspiring against the public interest. Without having to match the effort of one outfit against another, neither an independent nor a governmental institution can operate efficiently. Like government, independent institutions are ineffective largely because they no longer compete.

The independent sector will grow strong again when its leaders realize that its unique, indispensable natural role in America is to compete with government. It must be as eager as government to take on new public problems. It must be imaginative, vigorous, persistent. Independent groups must line up in Washington, not begging for help but looking for bigger jobs to do.

Most important, acceptance of this competitive challenge will force the independent sector to use human resources fully and effectively, to put America's locked-up desire to serve to work again.

11

Accepting the
Competitive Challenge

When my co-workers and I first concluded that the independent sector could solve most pending public problems, we knew right away we would have to prove it, at least in a small way. People tend to think it would be nice if independent action could do big things, but believe it can't. They like alternatives to government action, but almost no one thinks the independent sector is going anywhere. They doubt that anybody can compete successfully with government.

Two years ago, a pollster asked the board members of a number of independent social agencies:

"Do you think private agencies should take more responsibility?"
Most of them said "Yes."
"Do you think they will?"
Most of them said "No."

The National Merit Scholarship Corporation, the biggest independent outfit in the scholarship business, threw in the towel with its 1961 annual report: "There will be a . . . relative shrinking of private scholarship funds. The role of government . . . will almost certainly increase." The Family Service Association of America says: "Voluntary family agencies cannot attempt to meet the need for a basic social service." In short, most people think reviving independent action sounds fine but won't work.

Clearly, we could only take the concept out of the sky with a concrete demonstration. So we decided to pick a problem and prove, by competing directly with government, that the independent sector could outperform the government sector.*

First we had to pick the battleground. We considered several. We thought of promoting a national network of low-cost nursing homes. We thought about financing college buildings, but found private financiers already pioneering effectively in this field. We looked at phases of urban redevelopment, some already tested in Indianapolis and in Knoxville. We wanted to find a problem big enough for our test to mean something, but small enough to give us a fighting chance to succeed with the limited money and people we could muster.

In the end, we settled on student loans. The federal government had only just moved into this field, with the National Defense Education Act of 1958, so its program wasn't deeply dug in. We had a hunch the independent sector could work dramatically on this particular problem.

First, we had to define the need with some precision. Who, exactly, needed how much help? "Expert" estimates of how much money students needed ranged from zero to billions. Some argued that students didn't need loans at all, while others said students wouldn't borrow money for college, or if they did, would never pay it back. Others said a lot of loan money was begging for takers. We took pains

* I was working for a foundation at the time, the William Volker Fund, whose board and especially whose president, Harold W. Luhnow, gave me a very free hand. They put up with many failures and costly mistakes, and deserve, along with the men who did the daily work, most of the credit for the independent enterprise we built together.

to look at all the facts we could find, leaning heavily on Dr. W. W. Hill, Jr., the pioneer student credit expert in Indianapolis. When we had sorted out data and assumptions, it looked like this:

> The problem was real. College costs were going up. More and more lower-income people were sending their children to college, and many had a desperate time paying the bills all at once. Long-term loans were a solid and tested answer. Since a college education adds greatly to a student's earning power, it makes sense for him to borrow capital to obtain this increase. We found proof that college students are exceedingly good credit risks. If the loan is formal and the repayment plan systematic, there are almost no losses.
>
> We estimated, perhaps conservatively, that the national demand for loans would tend to level off when 25 per cent of the students borrowed about 25 per cent of their total college costs.
>
> We knew commercial lenders eventually would meet a lot of this demand, through the rapidly growing programs which lent money to the parents of college students, and through the expanded practice of refinancing mortgages to tap savings.
>
> But we also found that the neediest students, whose parents had exhausted their ability to help, had the most trouble getting bank loans. A bank couldn't justify a no-collateral loan to a teen-age student who didn't work regularly. If a bank examiner found that kind of paper in the vault, he would probably lock the doors and call the police.

When we'd finished our analysis, we were convinced we had found a problem needing solution. The commercial sector couldn't fully solve it with the instruments at hand. The question became: How could the independent sector get this job done?

It would be dramatic if I could say we sat down and invented the ingenious method the independent sector now uses to solve this problem. But we didn't. Someone had already invented it.

Several years before, the bankers in Massachusetts had seen the problem, worked out a way to solve it, and put it to use. They saw no need for any grand new lending agency. They just made it possible for existing banks to lend to the neediest students. They formed a nonprofit corporation to guarantee bank loans to needy college students. They got gifts from companies, foundations, and individuals to provide a fund to support the guarantee. Banks all over the state signed up to make low-cost, long-term loans available to any Massachusetts student who needed to borrow money for college and whose college would say he was likely to finish the course of study he had started. The system—first conceived, I'm told, by a turkey farmer—worked beautifully.

This Massachusetts plan had spread slowly to other states: New York State had started a plan, using tax money; Maine had an independent plan; Rhode Island had one, and so did other states. We decided that if the guarantee method could be put to work promptly all across the country, we could solve the student loan problem. So we set up a nonprofit corporation, United Student Aid Funds, Inc., with this goal:

> To make it possible for any deserving college student in the nation to borrow money at a bank in his neighborhood with no collateral other than a promising academic record.

We were determined to do it independently—without any government help. We employed a distinguished management consultant firm, Arthur D. Little and Company of Cambridge, Massachusetts, to help us figure out the operating details. We tested the program for a year in one state, Indiana, and then studied that experience carefully and made a number of changes in the program—some big and some small. For example, we found our forms were too complicated. So we made them simple.

The modified program works like this: Banks sign contracts with us, agreeing to lend $12.50 at a nonprofit rate for every dollar we hold in a security fund. We get this fund partly as deposits from colleges and universities and partly from foundation and business grants.

Colleges tell us which students need to borrow and how much they need. The banks make and collect the loans. A student may borrow up to $1,000 a year in any undergraduate year (freshmen temporarily excepted) and $2,000 in any graduate year, up to an over-all total of $4,000. He begins to repay four months after he graduates, and he has three to four years to repay, depending on how much he has borrowed.

Why did we do it just this way? We wanted to fill any gaps left by existing private programs, but we didn't want to replace these programs. We wanted to combine the abilities of four groups—students, banks, colleges, contributors—so we could meet the real needs of students at the lowest possible cost. We wanted a plan automatically self-adjusting to any level of need. We wanted to meet the total need for low-cost loans.

Then we began to sell. It was slow going at first, partly because the scheme was new, but partly because of awkward salesmanship. Some banks were very receptive, others reluctant. Some banks signed quickly, others thought we were Bolsheviki who should be spurned if not suppressed. The tide turned for us when California's Bank of America, world's biggest bank, signed up after intensive probing. At first the colleges couldn't believe we were on the level—that we could give them a line of credit of $25,000 for $1,000 deposited with us, that they could get their money back if their needs declined, and that their duties were limited to filling out one simple form for each student applicant. It sounded like patent medicine. And fund-raising was difficult. The program was untested. Worst of all, donors felt the government had already pre-empted the field. It was a hard sale all around.

By the end of the first year of national operation we had only 944 banks, 37 colleges. We had made only 3,000 loans totaling $2.2 million. Then business began to pick up. By the end of the second year we had 3,105 banks, 464 colleges and had made 16,000 loans totaling $8.6 million.

As I write this, we've operated the national program a little over three years. We have 5,500 banks in 49 states, 685 colleges. The corporation has guaranteed 68,000 loans totaling $40 million. We have nearly reached our goal. This year we are doing business at an annual rate of $40 million and can, we feel certain, expand rapidly to meet any level of demand that may emerge. Now that the savings and loan associates are moving firmly into this field, using our independent re-insurance, the commercial banks face lively competition. My hope is that a profit-seeking re-insurance agency will soon give USA Funds some competitive pressure from the commercial side.

Meanwhile, we've watched our federal competitor expand rapidly. Its "temporary" program, in theory passed as a stopgap until private resources could tool up for the job, mushroomed. The first year, it lent $30 million. This year, it is lending $163.3 million. It once declared that it would lend $275 million in 1971.

The federal program works like this: the government advances money to the colleges. They re-lend it to the students, and collect the loans. Students begin to repay a year after they graduate and repayment can take up to ten years. The student pays no interest while he's in school. He pays 3 per cent while he's repaying the loan. Students can borrow more than they can under our private plan, and the program includes freshmen. If the student trains for certain favored professions, as much as half his loan is forgiven.

Already the superiority of the independent program is evident. Dollars invested in our program (because of our multiplier and the faster turnover) do nearly fifty times the work of dollars put into the federal program. The "low" federal interest rate is an illusion. It ignores the colleges' large handling costs, which in our program are borne by the bank. We have calculated that the average student borrower pays $207 less interest under the federal program than under ours, but it costs the college at least $482.50 to make this $207 saving possible. The college could easily afford to grant the $275.50 difference to the borrower or some other needy student.

The more "liberal" federal terms—low interest and extended repayments—don't benefit anybody. They simply encourage delinquencies. No one knows for sure how many government loans are delinquent. As this is written, the number at Boston College is a scandalous 40 per cent. In 1964, a survey of a thousand colleges by the General Accounting Office revealed a 16.6 per cent delinquency, ten times the rate on similar commercial loans and almost twenty times the delinquency rate of USA Funds' borrowers.

For years, needy college students were denied credit because lenders thought, erroneously, that students were bad credit risks. It took years to establish the credit reputation of students. Now a carelessly conceived federal program is rapidly destroying the needy student's strongest weapon in his battle to pay his college bill.

Responsible government officials have grown more and more anxious about the federal program. It is becoming clear that student lending is best done by the practiced hands of bankers, and that our guarantee approach is the sounder method. As we were more and more often called to Washington to discuss our experience, we began to feel our program was gaining recognition in high places.

We were too right. In 1964, Senator Vance Hartke proposed a bill which would substitute a federal guarantee program for our private one. The Senator cited our experience as evidence that his plan would work. In other words, not only should the government do what independent institutions can't do, it should also do what they can. We testified that such a substitution was unnecessary, if not unkind, and begged for time to show more fully what we could do. The bill didn't go anywhere.*

But in his 1965 State of the Union Message, President Johnson, without giving details, proposed the establishment of a federal guarantee program. We thought then that we were dead. We rushed to Washington, but without much hope. We talked to anybody who would listen, in the Treasury, the Commerce Department, the Bureau of the Budget, and the Office of Education, and eventually the White House. Richard Goodwin, a top White House aide, took three hours to listen carefully to our case. The Office of Education people, who run the present program and who would run the proposed guarantee program, were, of course, dead against us. But elsewhere we got a cordial hearing.†

The officials we spoke to had naturally depended in the past on information from the Office of Education. So the other agencies knew little or nothing about what we and other non-federal institutions were doing and planned to do. They listened attentively to our story, studied the information we submitted carefully, requested more details.

When the President's Education Message went to the Congress, translating the generalities of the State of the

* Senator Hartke invited us to testify for his proposal. It was obvious that he expected our support. The desire to be relieved of responsibility has become so universal that the opposite impulse is simply not expected to appear.

† The Peace Corps even contracted through American Funds for private loans to its volunteers who happen to need credit for personal reasons.

Union Message into specifics, we were delighted. The President did not go on, as we had feared, with the idea of a federal guarantee program. He referred only to the need to encourage existing non-federal guarantee programs. We waited impatiently for the Administration's Education Bill, which further translates the President's recommendations into concrete legislative proposals. Again, we were relieved to find that the spirit of these recommendations was that the government would act only in places in which non-federal agencies demonstrably could not act.

The Bill was not, of course, all we had hoped for. The Office of Education succeeded in designating itself as the judge of whether or not we perform adequately. While we welcome open competition with government for this responsibility, we doubt the fairness of letting our competitor judge the race. So we hope Congress will not permit the Office of Education to usurp this legislative responsibility.

The final chapters of this story aren't yet written. The Office of Education may persuade Congress we are incompetent. Some combination of federal programs may displace our program. On the other hand, Congress may one day find commercial and independent agencies able to the whole job—and more.

But whatever the result, certain things are clear. Our decision to compete with government was sound, and we were right to keep at it. Public policy will be more sensible because our organization competes with government. This competition is good for us: the federal government is a tough competitor. Since we can't hope to match its blunt ability to pour cash directly on the problem, we have to compete on other terms. We are forced to use a dramatically more efficient method, which uses a little seed money and a few independent staffers to mobilize thousands of skilled professionals directly to work on the problem—with resources of the commercial sector that are ultimately far greater. Government has money in abundance, but the independent sector has a much more important resource—oceans of talent—and the greater opportunity to trigger the commercial sector into action.

Our competitive presence is good discipline for government. Congress can compare our costs of operation, our default experience, and our estimates of need, can sort out this complicated problem, and write sounder public policy. How, for example, would Congress know that a 16.6-percent delinquency rate is not normal for student loans if our experience were not available? The federal program has nine district offices. We have one small national office in New York. How else would Congress know that a loan program doesn't need district offices?

In short, we believe our modest experiment has confirmed our hunch that competition with government is not only legitimate but necessary, and that the discipline this competition imposes on the independent sector is the key to the recovery of its lost vitality. We would have made several mistakes, and served students less well, had we not been determined to top government's record.

Moreover, we believe that in the process, we discovered how to compete with government. We stumbled onto some principles which may provide a general strategy for competitive independent action. They are described in the next chapter.

12

How to Compete
with Government

Competition with government is really a competition for the confidence of the American people. As we saw in Chapter 10, we send representatives to Congress to decide for us what the public business is and who shall do it. Government's recent growth means simply that it has been able to convince Congress that it can perform better than independent or commercial institutions. The independent sector is clearly failing in this competition. It fails for two reasons. Either:

(1) it has left some important piece of public business undone or poorly done

                    or

(2) it has done a good job but has failed to get its story across to the public and its representatives in Congress.

Thus, the independent sector's competitive problem is very much like the competitive problem businesses face every morning. And businesses, to compete effectively, have to do four things:

(1) Find out what people want.
(2) Develop a product to meet that demand.

(3) Produce it economically.

(4) Sell it vigorously.

The independent sector needs to do the same things:

(1) *Research:* to find real human needs, their extent, their cause.

(2) *Development:* to find the best ways the independent sector can meet these needs.

(3) *Mobilization:* to get the independent sector to adopt these new methods.

(4) *Information:* to sell what it accomplishes to the public.

In a simpler America, this wasn't necessary. We could see needs and remedies more easily. But today we can't see the public business so clearly. We have to take problems apart and look hard to find their cures. We have to plan carefully. We have to use up-to-date production methods, and often must create new organizational machinery. We have to report the results systematically to the public.

RESEARCH

The government is quick to perceive emerging human needs. It is never stuck for a solution. This is as it should be. In a complex society, we would overlook many public problems if someone weren't looking for them. But, predictably, people who push federal programs often present biased evidence. They tend to exaggerate our problems. They say these problems are caused by factors only the government can fix. They understate what anybody else is doing and can do.

Author John Steinbeck, a man with a practiced eye for human misery, drove across America lately to see how we were doing. In a splendid book, *Travels With Charley* (Viking, 1963), he gave a generally favorable report. He found a friendly, if restless, nation of good people. Aside from heart-sickening racial turmoil, we seemed to be doing all right.

But officially, we are on the brink of moral, economic, and cultural collapse. We are in deep statistical distress.

Our unemployment rate is dangerously high.

Our growth rate has been dangerously low.

We need thousands more public school classrooms, and the situation is getting worse.

One fourth of us live in abject poverty.

Most older people can't get decent medical care.

By 2000, we will need three times as many places to play as we have now.

We need thousands more engineers, teachers, physicists, social workers, and recreationists right now.

Such "official" figures, fortunately, tell us only where the hard sell is on. Federal statistics often depend less on human need than on what is needed to make a political sale. President Roosevelt pioneered the system: he saw "one-third of the nation ill-housed, ill-clad, ill-nourished." Donald Richberg, who worked with Roosevelt on the speech, tells us where the figure came from. Richberg, reporting on their work together over the text in his autobiography *My Hero* (G. P. Putnam's Sons, 1954), said, "I protested that there were no statistics which could possibly be marshalled to support such a statement. . . . I ventured to suggest that if one were going to pull a figure out of the sky, it would at least be safer to say one-fourth. . . . But F.D.R. had a certain feeling for numbers. . . . He liked the one-third and he wasn't particularly bothered by using a fraction which, even if it could not be supported, could not be disproved."

These days, political statistics are worked up much more carefully. For example:

Congress recently passed a program to help colleges. They had been told: Between 1960 and 1970, college enrollment will double. We face a national emergency. "There are simply not enough classrooms, laboratories, or libraries for the rising flood of applicants. Nothing less is at stake than our national strength, progress and survival."

Only the federal government can do the job.

If these things are really true, could Congress fail to assign responsibility to government?

But many experts doubt these facts. Researcher Roger Freeman of Stanford's Hoover Institution points out that college enrollment will not grow as fast in the eight years beginning 1962 as it did in the eight years before 1962. A researcher for the Fund for the Advancement of Education says, "If classrooms were used to the greatest extent possible . . . present classrooms could handle four times the number of students." Journalists Benjamin Fine and Sidney Eisenberg polled 3,000 schools; 795 reported vacancies.

We are told one in twenty workers can't find a job. So we need a bigger federal job program. But the figures include:

- people who have quit their jobs to look for better ones,
- people who can't work for a while because other workers are on strike,
- people looking for part-time jobs,
- seasonal workers,
- handicapped people who can't work.

Many economists think that fewer than a million people are having real trouble finding a suitable job.

Government figures now tell us a fourth of our people still live in poverty. No doubt many do. But according to *Fortune*'s Edmund V. Faltermayer, if we applied the same yardstick to Britain, we would find that three fourths of the British are poor. Opinion analyst Samuel Lubell writes: "The statistics being used of the people who are supposed to be living in poverty are not good figures at all." An honest concern for the poor does not justify imaginary statistics to scare off non-government competitors in the public business of helping the poor.

After World War II, federal spokesmen said we were starving small business. Congress passed new federal props for small business. A University of Chicago economist studied the problem, and found that small business could get capital as easily as big business.

The government sector's boosters overstate public problems. They also say problems have causes only the government can remedy. And government often reasons backward —from remedy to cause. Government can move resources around. It can tax and spend. It can restrict and punish. But our most urgent new public problems can't be solved with such crude instruments.

The President's Science Advisory Committee says that while we turned out twenty-nine hundred Ph.D.s in 1950, we will need thousands more by 1970. The Committee says we must subsidize scientists. Yet since personal commitment is more important than money to a real scientist, *Science* magazine says subsidies "may diminish the number of gifted individuals with the necessary motivation to be truly creative." At least one venerable foundation, with a time-tested skill at cultivating scientific genius, is near despair over the government's heavy hand.

Most experts agree that if you have to pick one cause, bad family life is the prime contributor to juvenile crime. But federal programs are entirely "based on the belief that obstacles to economic and social betterment among low income groups are the main cause of delinquency." Why does the government sector focus a one-track mind on this diagnosis when the evidence points another way? You can "better" people economically by spending money. You can't improve family life or the community that fosters better family life that way.

The federal government is "solving" the farm problem with bewildering and costly price supports. But as we have seen, the marginal farmers, who were the public reason for the program, grow only 9 per cent of the farm products sold.

The problems of education? The government says the schools need money. But many education experts disagree. "Education is weak, but it is not undernourished," writes Ernest van den Haag. "It is weak partly from obesity, partly from faulty diet, and above all, from lack of exercise." And the late Beardsley Ruml, liberal inventor of pay-as-you-go income taxes, wrote, "New money is not needed in anything like the amounts presently estimated. Many of the necessary funds are already at the disposal of the colleges, but are being dissipated through wastes in the curriculum and in methods of instruction."

Nor do the government sector's advocates waste much time boosting their competition. They often look briefly at the commercial and independent sectors. These are, they almost always find, "inadequate."

Early in his administration, President Eisenhower told his Secretary of Health, Education and Welfare to find out what non-governmental agencies could do to give older people the medical care they needed. The Department got to work. Several months later they reported. Their search for voluntary solutions was "futile." You can imagine how hard federal employees looked for a program that wouldn't require any federal employees.

Clearly the independent sector needs a broad-scale research effort of its own, if only to give itself the courage to try. It cannot use government figures in setting its goals and programs. We can't leave real needs unmet, but neither can we afford to waste real energy solving imaginary problems or problems of imaginary dimensions. We need to search, in our communities and in the nation, for human distress. We need to find out who is in what kind of trouble and why. We need to know what independent institutions are doing and what they could do. We need to know what, if anything, holds back independent—and commercial—potential.

The independent sector should look for problems before they ripen. We need an early warning system. A critic said of a liberal politician, "He has [government] solutions for problems we don't even have yet." So should the independent sector.

The commercial sector spends millions looking for new markets, getting ready for new demands. The government sector spends millions looking for new items of public business. The independent sector spends next to nothing. Yet of the three, it knows least about its own strength and how and where and when to put it to work.

DEVELOPMENT

As the independent sector develops its own sense of what needs to be done in modern America, it must then work out specific ways to act. The basic know-how is at hand. In response to the increasingly technical requirements of business and government, a whole new industry, the research and development industry, has sprung up. These organizations, some commercial but many independent, will, it seems, tackle anything—from the economic planning of Disneyland to the launching of Telstar. They know how to find answers. We are beginning to discover how to ask the questions.

New ways to use physical materials could revolutionize independent action, just as they have revolutionized commercial production and distribution. We can see some results already.

One researcher designed a round hospital. He claims it can cut costs in half. Others have developed hospital beds which work electrically. They pay for themselves in two years in saved nurses' time. Intercoms save 15 per cent of the nurses' trips to patients. A $5,000 analyzer frees two $4,000 employees for other duties. Ultrasonic devices to clean equipment would save $19.5 million each year, if all hospitals used them. Throw-away syringes for injections save 25 per cent of the cost, add to safety.

A builder in Detroit designed apartments for poor older people and rented them for $22 a month. In the cultural field, new know-how in electronics, plastics, and optics can sharply cut down the cost of staging an opera.

These achievements promise even larger ones, as R&D technology is systematically focused on the problems of independent institutions, but there is a much larger challenge. For the independent sector's great crime is not that it wastes things, but that it wastes people.

I have a friend in San Francisco who is a brilliant young lawyer. He works hard and is rising rapidly in the profession. He has a deep sense of community obligation. He does almost anything he is asked to do. But what are his assignments? He sells Christmas trees on a drafty lot during the holidays. He begs for money from his friends for "good" causes, and like all of us, hates it. He sits through tedious committee meetings which, as a rule, decide only when the committee will meet again. He finds little joy or satisfaction in these activities. But, more important, a fine specialized talent is wasted on chores a child could do as well.

The commercial sector's energy exploded because it released the energy of people, discovered their most valuable specialty, and put them to work at it. In Detroit, a man takes his place on the line, does a job he can understand and handle, and contributes in combination with thousands of other specialists to the production of a car he couldn't build by himself in a thousand years. His work has been organized for him, and his productivity multiplies.

The independent sector has not learned how to use people. There are millions of people longing to be called to service. But there is no longer much they can do. We have professionalized the independent sector's work force. All the citizen can do is pay or persuade others to pay. Experts, we are told, must find the jobs for the hard-core unemployed. Only trained people can deal with juvenile crime. Only social workers can help troubled families.

So we cut off an army of talented people. Lay people, say the specialists, can raise money, sell Christmas trees, and lick stamps, but they can't, as they once took a hammer and helped raise a barn, deal directly with modern problems. Economist Solomon Fabricant points to a "displacement of voluntary work by professional service." We are, of course, supposed to be short of all kinds of professionals. But there are millions of willing lay people who aren't thought fit to do the work. We've drawn a curtain of professionalism between the citizen and the public business.

Thus, the great potential of the independent sector is bottled up. Its energy is reduced to a trickle that is forced through the narrow professional funnel.

And here, I think, is the key to effective competition with government. We found it accidentally when we built the United Student Aid Funds program. We were determined to compete with government. We could not hope even to match government by imitating its methods. We hadn't the power to raise hundreds of millions of dollars annually for direct loans. We were forced to find a way that used very little new money. Our slender corporation simply provided a mechanism through which the talent of thousands of existing individuals and institutions were put to new work. We defined the task of each participant carefully. We mobilized each group for a responsibility which matched its experience and skill. The strength of the program lies in this painstaking distribution of responsibility among students, banks, colleges and universities, and contributors. We found the trigger to release such a torrent of energy that it surprised us as much as anybody.

But this was only a small, experimental beginning. Beyond lies a boundless research challenge: How can the vast stockpile of specialized human ingenuity and skill be put to work on modern problems?

Many unusually enterprising individuals, moved by deep concern and guided by common sense, find satisfying roles for themselves. New York publisher Lyle Stuart was disturbed one night in a Brooklyn library by a noisy street gang. When he complained, he found out they had nowhere else to go, had no adult leadership. He won their confidence, learned they wanted jobs, helped them in their search.

As a result, Harrison Salisbury reported in the *New York Times:*

> The roughhouse gang that used to disrupt the library has vanished. The youngsters are working afternoons and Saturdays. There is still plenty of delinquency at Fort Greene, and gang problems as well. Not all of Mr. Stuart's boys will be straight. But a warm heart, common sense and civic responsibility have done much.

Elmer L. Winter, president of Milwaukee-based Manpower, Inc., heard that many young people in the Milwaukee area would probably be out of work in the summer months. He set up Youthpower, Inc., donated an office, typewriters, and office supplies, and helped it decide what to do. In a few weeks Youthpower found summer jobs for over a thousand boys and girls. Mr. Winter probably knows more about part-time employment than anybody in America. Probably no one else could have put Youthpower together.

Several months ago I lunched with Dr. Cuthbert Hurd, chairman of the Computer Usage Company. Dr. Hurd has a hunch computers can help us get fast national reports on jobs for people who are out of work. He's set aside several days a month of his own time to find out how.

At a banquet in New York last year, I sat next to the head of a major casualty insurance company. Knowing that teen-age drivers often can't buy commercial liability insurance and have to be covered by state government insurance, he spent a lot of time and money to figure out how private insurance could be sold to teen-agers. He found how the safer risks could be sorted out. He now sells this insurance on a nonprofit basis, cutting down the need for government to do it—and serving people who will soon be profitable adult customers.

To open up jobs for teen-agers in New Rochelle, businessman Boris Feinman set up Paycheck, Inc., beginning with a parking lot and a flower cart. He plans to do much more.

In 1958 in Phoenix, Richard K. Steinman, who heads a chain of small loan companies, set up Family Debt Counselors to help families get out of debt. He knew the problem intimately and he knew how to do something about it. By 1965, similar services will help families in eighty other communities.

In Hazleton, Pennsylvania, Dr. Ed Dessen saw his town on the skids as its mines shut down. He set up CANDO to attract new industry. In five years, CANDO had created eleven thousand new jobs.

None of these men are professional social workers. They are laymen, exercising their independent responsibility with unusual conscientiousness. They invest their time in public service carefully and imaginatively, matching their particular skills to problems at hand.

But such enterprisers are, in the nature of things, rare. Most of us have the same impulse which moves them, but need guidance in how our particular skills can best be applied to the problems we see about us. "What can I do?"

people ask. I can imagine no more urgent research task than to find answers.

Bold innovation in methods of organizing the service impulse has become as important to the independent sector as assembly-line production and the corporate form of organization were to the commercial sector. I can only guess what forms these innovations will take. They will not be developed abstractly, but, I expect, will develop as effective competition with government makes them increasingly necessary.

Some general prospects are clear. For example, the franchising principle, so widely used in commerce, seems uniquely adaptable to some of the independent sector's unfinished business. Franchising blends central expertise with local initiative and responsibility. The Sears Foundation, in a project mentioned earlier, has pioneered this principle. Any determined rural community that needs and wants a team of doctors and a clinic can get expert guidance from the Foundation at every step of the way. But initiative and responsibility rest wholly with the community itself.

DATA International in Palo Alto, California, is pioneering in another promising technique. This organization keeps a careful skill bank, with which technicians of all types all over the country register. Simultaneously, DATA encourages people working abroad to ask for help with their problems. As these are reported, DATA assigns them to technicians who know how to help. Assignments have ranged from construction of chicken houses in Indonesia to ridding tomatoes of fungus to the development of a telephone exchange in Turkey. But DATA's principle—that specialized skills should be systematically linked up to specific problems—doubtless has a much wider application.

The independent sector obviously has a staggering development job to do. But the skills needed to get it done are there, waiting to be put to work.

MOBILIZATION

As the independent sector develops new and better ways of applying its energy to the public business, it will find, as we did in student loans, that these plans will have to be promoted skillfully and persistently. Peter G. Peterson, president of Bell and Howell, has long wanted to apply the hard sell of commerce to worthy educational projects.

As we have seen in Chapter 7, the sector now works unevenly. Institutions don't adopt tested methods quickly. Commercial organizations are always on the lookout for better ways to do things. Competitors force them to adopt new methods promptly. News of new and better practices spreads fast through thousands of trade magazines and bulletins.

But independent groups don't copy new methods. The know-how often stays at its point of origin. Look at Saul Alinsky's conquest of America's worst slum, at Henry Viscardi's success in putting the handicapped to work, at Cleo Blackburn's work in rebuilding slums, at the Menningers' work in mental health, at Millard Roberts' work in education. These operations rarely reach far beyond what these gifted and strong-willed men can do themselves.

In commerce it's different. Edison lighted not only Menlo Park but the whole world. Ford put a whole nation behind the wheel of the Model T. But the independent sector doesn't copy sound practices automatically.

Building United Student Aid Funds taught us this lesson. The hardest job was to sell the program to the banks and colleges. We didn't invent anything. We stole the idea from Massachusetts. And we wasted a lot of time at first waiting for people to buy it from our brochures. We began to move only when we began to sell. We found that the independent sector doesn't get going without a lot of pushing. But we also found that determined people can mobilize it.

There are some striking isolated illustrations of effective mobilization of the independent sector. I was deeply impressed by the polio immunization program as it was handled in our county. The coverage was nearly total. The program was beautifully planned. The press, radio, and television played their part. The medical society pitched in to man the immunization stations. Hundreds of volunteers handled the crowds, and were so skillfully briefed that there were few hitches, even though several hundred thousand people were involved. We were asked as we left to put a quarter in a can if we wanted to, more if we chose, or nothing. When the books were closed, there was a surplus of nearly $100,000. I served on a committee that distributed the surplus among local charities.

But examples like this are rare. The independent sector has not, on the whole, learned to mobilize its resources promptly and sensibly. This lethargy will be cured to some extent when the independent sector's competitive spirit is restored. But in the modern world, salesmanship is a permanent imperative. Those who think the independent sector will be restored if we simply collect "good ideas" and print bulletins about them are in for heartbreak. We can no longer vaguely admonish independent institutions to "do better." Nor can we expect national action from magazine articles titled "What Cucamonga Can Do Your Town Too Can Do."

Government uses tax money to buy talent. And this method requires much less promotional and organizational skill than does persuading independent individuals and institutions to work more effectively. However, competitive pressure has developed in the commercial sector a breed of gifted promoters and organizers of commercial action. We need to create such a breed in the independent sector. They are our scarcest resource.

INFORMATION

To compete with government and win, you have to perform. But that's not enough; you also have to let the public know you're performing. Government is the master huckster of its plans and programs. The independent sector— humble and reticent, mute and invisible—has been no good at all. The public forgets it exists.

This is, in part, natural. The groups which are good at getting things done are often no good at politics. The groups best at getting results—Alcoholics Anonymous, for example—shun publicity, spurn outside money, and go quietly about helping such people as alcoholics. Our best writers avoid the spotlight. Our poor ones hire people to keep them in it.

The people who do the country's work keep busy at it. Others talk to Congress about what they could do with more money and more power. Some people like to work; other people like to talk. Neither group is good at what the other does well.* So it isn't natural for the independent sector to crow about what it does, to sell itself. Its institutions are scattered. They speak with no single voice. But they must find ways to overcome reticence, to find a single voice and to amplify it in public debate.

The press has become passive. The initiative has largely been reversed. You don't find the press looking for news as much as you find news looking for the press. Those who go after attention get it; those who don't, don't. Thus, while the press reports what goes on in commerce and

---

* In any field in which you can get ahead with talk rather than results, you can observe the differing habits of the workers and the talkers. The worker hates committee meetings; the talker would rather meet than eat. The worker doesn't like to talk about how he gets his work done; the talker talks constantly about techniques he rarely practices. The worker hardly ever complains of overwork; the talker is always over his head in "work." I don't know why exactly, but the worker tends to speak plain English, while the talker speaks a kind of baroque and redundant prose. The worker is modest about what he'll get done; the talker is completely immodest about what he'll do tomorrow.

government, it neglects what the independent sector does. For example, at the time the press hailed the Peace Corps as a bold innovation, 33,000 Americans, sponsored mainly by religious groups, were working quietly on a voluntary basis in 146 countries, doing the same things in the same places we were planning to send the Peace Corpsmen. These groups had been at it since 1809.

The sector of American society Tocqueville thought most important has become largely invisible and inaudible. The press covers golf more fully than independent action —partly because the independent sector doesn't do much new work, but partly because it doesn't make noise.

Again, a competitive posture will force a new realism about the independent sector's public and political relations. For years, Ford proudly refused to advertise. He thought the merit of his product was manifest and advertising superfluous, if not degrading. But as you may have noticed, competition in time forced him to advertise.

In political relations, the independent sector has some special problems. Clearly, the federal bureaucracy's convenient monopoly on the ear of Congress will be hard to break. There is virtually no limit on the bureaucracy's access to Congress. But independent institutions, if tax-exempt, cannot legally appear before Congress in pursuit of new responsibility or to beg that responsibility not be wrested from them. It is imperative that the right of the independent sector to defend itself and to seek new responsibility be clearly affirmed.

I would go further. I've proposed elsewhere that Congress establish an office, similar to the General Accounting Office, charged to inform Congress systematically of the achievements and potential of non-governmental institutions. Like the GAO, this agency would be responsible only to Congress, thus independent of the executive. It could help Congress perform its natural function by performing the role of the public defender and advocate of the independent sector, making certain it was fairly and vigorously defended. Such an agency would best be financed by private funds.

Here, then, are the elements of a strategy for independent action. It must find out for itself what needs to be done in America, develop modern answers to modern problems, mobilize, and tell the public what it's doing. The next chapters speculate on how a few of our principal independent institutions might put this strategy to work in specific ways.

✳

13

Business and the
Public Business

✳

A restless spirit moves among businessmen. They employ a clumsy language about "corporate citizenship," "company responsibility to the community," and even "stewardship." Such talk is, of course, not new, but it is gaining a fierce and significant intensity, more in private than in public. Some businessmen worry over an apparent conflict of values. Proud of a tough-minded approach to profits and aware that they cannot be social workers with shareholder money, they are on the prowl for an underlying idea that is missing.

What causes this concern? The businessman's desire for meaningful service, I believe, is pushing against inadequate machinery through which to function. He has the will but does not see the way. In this uneasy mood, the U.S. business community is the group most likely to trigger a renaissance of the independent sector.

Many reach instinctively in this direction. In city after city, when you look carefully, you find businessmen leading a strong resurgence of private charities. They have led most of the successful urban renewal efforts since Pittsburgh's Golden Triangle. But few sense the effectiveness of their own efforts. The traditional rhetoric of "private charity" reminds them that they are not John D. Rockefellers; they fail to see that with proper organization and tactics, they have far greater resources than businessmen had in the days when a few financial giants dominated the economy. Today's businessmen don't really know their own strength. So, even while working to prevent it, most are resigned to an ever greater government monopoly on public service.

They hear urgent warnings. In an echo of Tocqueville, Donald David, as an officer of the Ford Foundation, said, "I am convinced that if private enterprise philanthropy were to abdicate to government, private business would follow not too far behind."

But businessmen are not sure they can respond to the warnings. More than any other group, they are victimized by the "public-private" division of all U.S. life. It traps them. So long as we view society as a two-part system, business is exposed to a direct, losing battle with government. The profit discipline becomes a fatal handicap rather than an essential strength. Only when you understand the important array of institutions that are neither commercial nor governmental, but provide a buffer between the two, do you understand how the American dream once combined the ideals of freedom and welfare. Since the decline of this decisive force, business has paid a high price in regulation, taxes and public ill will. And as of 1965, the future of the commercial sector depends upon the re-emergence of a vital independent sector.

The present situation arose from the uneven growth of the three sectors in this incredible twentieth century. With the rise of national corporations and the mass-production line, the nation and its problems became for a while more centralized. The Kentucky farmer who went to work in Detroit found his family much more vulnerable to general economic conditions over which he had no control. The expansionist vitality of commerce was not, however, matched in the independent sector. For one thing, independent action had always been more of a personal instinct than a deliberate program, accidental rather than organized. Responsible local businessmen, in direct touch with their communities, had long engaged in activities that could never be explained by the abstract version of the profit motive. They had, through the church and other agencies, been sweeping up after commerce for generations. But nobody since Tocqueville had really understood how the job was done.

The Depression demonstrated the consequences. In spite of their archaic machinery, the private welfare groups under business leadership made an heroic, little-remembered stand against overwhelming odds. In Chicago, businessman Sewell Avery, later to become a tragic figure at Montgomery Ward, led the commercial community's determined drive to keep up the pay for teachers, policemen and social workers. In Kansas City, furniture-maker William Volker slashed executive salaries and rode out the crash without laying off a single employee.

In Seattle, the Community Fund contributions told a story of courage and despair: contributions rose from $190,000 in 1925 to $304,000 in 1931, then quadrupled to $1,221,-000 in the grim year ending September 30, 1932. In 1933, when exhausted citizens gave up and left the job to the New Deal, the fund fell back to $199,000. Private charity became, to the New Dealers, an object of derision.

So business lost its silent partner. Businessmen, their confidence battered, fought to regain their position in the national community by ideological argument with politicians. They wrongly assumed that freedom is won by debate. They failed to see that the liberal politician's debating advantage lies not in his philosophy but in his habit of proposing specific action for specific problems. Do something, even if it's wrong, is a natural human reaction to crisis. Traditional economic theory, for all its wisdom, did not provide business with a positive answer to proposals for government action. It is hard to persuade a hungry man to wait for Adam Smith's "invisible hand" to deliver food. Without strong agencies to attack human needs directly, business left government with the only visible hand ready to help. In dismay, business spent a lot of breath, time, and money to defend itself. Much of the effort was devoted to internal communications, preaching to each other at luncheons and conventions.

In its efforts to reach the public, business turned to homespun economic and political principles. Business groups hired ad men to lavish their talents on tricky ways to tell the advantages of free enterprise. The clinching appeal in most of these pitches about "the American way of life" was a recitation of our superior number of refrigerators, cars, washing machines, and bathtubs. The conservative propagandists with whom I worked in this painful period used to laugh about the "bathtub economics" that had become our stock in trade.

Most of us sensed that we weren't getting the message across. We didn't really need William H. Whyte, Jr., of *Fortune* to write his searing book on business propaganda. His title: *Is Anybody Listening?* His conclusion: No. He was right. If we had been trying to sell soap rather than an idea, we would have faced up to the fact that something fundamental was wrong with our whole strategy. Instead, we tended to do what business can never do: we blamed the customers. Each time the public accepted a federal program, we bewailed the ignorance of the very voters we had been "educating" with all our skill and zeal.

The bathtub-economics approach failed simply because it was irrelevant. The public, in spite of the Depression, never lost its general belief in capitalism's productive efficiency, and recent years of prosperity have strongly re-affirmed that faith. Even the Russians, still bent on burying private enterprise, have been forced into reluctant experiments with capitalistic concepts. If we have the imagination to act wisely, we may yet see the clear triumph of a rejuvenated capitalism in the world.

So why didn't the productive efficiency of business answer the challenge raised by governmental proposals? Simply because business could not respond to specific problems with specific action. When federal statisticians dramatized the poverty of Appalachia last year and argued for an aid program, business had no way to make an alternative bid for reviving the region.

The business position became ironic. Each new proposal for federal action or regulation came in the form of a demand for improvement of existing efforts. "We are not repealing free enterprise," says NAM President W. P. Gullander. "We are improving it to death." The business community worried about the taxes that stunted its growth and the regulations that made it rigid. It fought these taxes and regulations directly, but it was fighting the effect and not the cause. Congress did not tax and regulate business just for the hell of it or because it wanted to punish businessmen. In the depths of the Depression, some federal activists became anti-business bigots, but this derisive tactic did not remain a popular issue. The real problem has been the public's inability to see anything but government as the instrument for deliberate, nonprofit betterment of the society.

To the businessman, the situation became all the more painful when he realized the extent of his social contribution strictly within his commercial function. Business is itself a welfare system. As the prime producer of goods and services, it provides abundantly for the general welfare. It has lifted the American standard of living to embarrassing heights compared to socialized nations, and it provides public services that dwarf government's contribution. From baseball to good books, from toys to ranch houses, the necessities and luxuries we take for granted are produced by private companies.

Let me illustrate. In September, 1964, a group of ten investor-owned utilities announced a $10.5-billion project to expand electric power in the nine Western states. It was a wholly commercial undertaking with no government financing involved. The project, when completed in 1986, will produce thirty-four thousand new jobs, $200 million in new payroll, $75 million in new tax revenue, and $75.2 million in new retail sales. This project was given scant notice in the press. Yet it will produce three times the power output of the Tennessee Valley Authority, which has, after a generation of sustained public attention, become a subject on which almost any citizen considers himself an expert advocate or critic.

The human "welfare" generated by these projects is surely the same, except the private project will be measurably more productive than TVA. Yet TVA was hailed as a great innovation, the other accorded about as much attention as the air we breathe.

When the government threatened to close its naval shipyard at Hunter's Point in San Francisco, the city fathers were horrified. But a study by John Lord King Associates, an alert architectural firm, showed that the conversion of the site to private industrial use would, in ten years, produce fourteen thousand new jobs, $100 million in new payrolls and $2.5 million in new local taxes. Normal business development would produce more "welfare" than the "essential" government project that long ago outlived its usefulness but had not, for lack of competitive pressure, undergone steady reform.

Commerce manages a lot of "public" enterprises skillfully. The Bell Telephone System is the best example. Travelers tell me that we have the world's best telephone service and the Western world's worst mail service. One is run by business; the other by government. In England, where the telephone is a subsidiary of the post office, the phones often work like Alexander Graham Bell's first models, and expansion-minded businesses often have to wait months for desperately needed service. One economic analyst is convinced that the failure of government-supplied communications is the main bottleneck to more rapid expansion of the European economy.

One hundred and forty-five million Americans have some form of commercial health insurance—up from forty-two million in 1946. Forty-three million workers are privately insured against disability. Ten million people age sixty-five and over—three out of five—have private medical insurance. Businesses build and lease college dormitories. Private developers renew cities. Jim Walter, the flamboyant shell-house pioneer, has put more low-income people in decent houses on a business basis than has any government project. When business operates "public" facilities—parking lots, parks—the costs are almost always lower and the service better; most important, the facility constantly renews itself to serve changing wants and demands.

A most dramatic example of commercial welfare came across my desk the other day. The foundation I direct had for several months been planning to develop a national chain of low-cost nursing homes. We studied in particular the methods of Holiday Inns, the very successful motel franchise, thinking that if nonprofit organizations could imitate their methods, we could provide nursing-home care at very low cost.

Then one day last March, I read in the *Wall Street*

Journal that Holiday Inns had formed a subsidiary to "operate a nation-wide system of franchised nursing homes, patterned somewhat after the motel chain." Their studies show that "reasonably priced, well-designed and economically built homes, under properly trained personnel, can render the service . . . at money-making prices." We had hoped, with our "welfare" project, to get the price-per-resident down to a rock-bottom $250 a month. Holiday Inn's probable price: $250 a month. For the old folks, which is welfare and which is not? The commercial entry into this badly needed public service reduced our role to a fraction of what I had expected it to be. One of my associates went to Holiday Inn executives to see if we could borrow their know-how to create a nonprofit system of homes for areas that would not be commercially profitable to them.

The nursing homes are no exception to the general rule. Businessmen constantly hunt for new markets by identifying a special need and then finding ways to meet it at lower cost than anybody else. In such effort, the profit motive often serves as an instrument rather than an original cause. This fact is hard to explain, because it contradicts the standard clichés. J. Irwin Miller, chairman of Cummins Engine Company, operates a highly profitable bank, the Irwin-Union Trust Company, in his home town of Columbus, Indiana. His bank outgrows any other in its Federal Reserve District because it constantly hunts for new financial services needed by people and institutions (especially churches) in its market area. "If you try to run a bank with the primary goal of making the biggest profit possible, you won't," says Miller. "But if you approach the operation of a bank from the point of view of how best it can serve the community, then the profits will follow."

To cynics, in and out of business, such remarks sound fatuous. But they may be nearer the truth than the rhetoric of profits as normally used. Time and again, the most successful businessmen are those who seek first to provide the best service and then work on the arithmetic of profit. Florida's George Jenkins, who has transformed his Publix Supermarkets into an expansive chain of pleasure domes for shoppers, broods about the competitors he has faced over the years. "If a man wants to be a good grocer, he can generally make a profit," muses Jenkins. "But these get-rich-quick fellows tend to lose their shirts."

Other businessmen, among them Chicago banker Gaylord A. Freeman, Jr., have developed a line of thought about the difference between short-term and long-term profits. If a professional manager tried to look good in each year's annual report by showing a dramatic profit, Freeman argues, he might be working against the interests of the shareholders. Their equity gains or loses value on the prospect for future profits, not just in the current annual report. So a real concern for the shareholder, says Freeman, could even justify a corporation investment in improving the society in ways that will provide a favorable climate for profits in the long run.

Such considerations tell more about the actual basis for business decisions than the standard arguments put forth by business propagandists. In fact, the strength of the industrial system may best be measured by its capacity to survive in spite of the case made for it by its most ardent advocates in the profit-only school. "Business acts better than it talks," says Irwin Miller. Business leaders have become impatient with the standard case, including bathtub economics, long made in their defense.

A strong new note has been struck of late. Over the past two years, trend-setters among business leaders have been searching for a sounder position. "Businessmen have won public confidence in the things for which they take responsibility," says Indiana's John Burkhart. "The trouble lies in areas where they have not taken responsibility." Men like Burkhart work toward a problem-solving approach and see the need to compete aggressively with government for solutions to public problems. Here are random quotes I gathered over a few months:

Lynn A. Townsend, President
Chrysler Corporation

"Business should take the initiative in exploring ways of filling the social needs of our country through non-governmental agencies and with the strong support of private enterprise."

———

Daniel Peterkin, Jr., President
Morton Salt Company

"We in business must assume leadership in solving some of the pressing economic problems both at home and abroad . . . the problems will not be solved unless we do . . . there will be no major breakthrough in business growth and earnings unless these problems are solved."

———

Daniel G. Wood
Steel industry public relations executive

"What I'm urging upon my fellow businessmen is to out-govern government. Let's identify problems and bring about solutions before the government is forced to act."

———

Elmer L. Winter, President
Manpower, Inc.

"We should not pass the ball to Washington . . . but should accept the challenge to demonstrate emphatically that American business and industry have the resources, vigor, intelligence and courage to meet the responsibilities of a free economy."

———

Bernard P. Gallagher
Marketing consultant

"Time is ripe for U.S. business to launch a mammoth program for social progress. . . . Prove that government centralism is not necessary. . . . Free enterprise can take the lead in meeting today's social and economic problems."

Charles A. Kothe, Vice-President
National Association of Manufacturers

"The only way to stop big government from getting bigger is for private industry, individuals and volunteer groups to do the jobs that need to be done—and do them better."

This new attitude is sweeping the business community, yet there is a danger that it will be frustrated for lack of an effective strategy. Clarence Francis, former chief of General Foods, is one of many wise veterans who abhor talk that is not followed by effective action. His worry is wise. If business continues to talk generally about what it should do and finds no way to do it, the talk will merely advertise the failure. What is needed is a machinery whereby business can identify real public problems, announce organized campaigns upon each, and then report accomplishments. It needs something it does not have, an essential supplement to what it can do under competitive discipline.

The best of this machinery lies in the independent sector. The reason is simple. Under the competitive system, even with the long-term view of profits, a single competitor assumes a handicap when he diverts time and money into non-revenue public service while his competitor does not. But under Tocqueville's "principle of association," individual and company competitors join together to share the responsibility and the cost. They not only act jointly, but in their mutual concern they constantly push each other into more effective personal action on local, state, and national levels.

The businessman's unique position is suggested by the fact that businessmen are the natural trustees of independent institutions. Businessmen, or their wives, make up majorities on the boards of most of our hospitals, colleges, and universities, and of most national and local health and welfare organizations. This situation, which occasionally leads to selfish misuse of private foundations, arises directly from the fact that our abundant production creates the extra margin of wealth that has always fed independent institutions. The American dream was realized in the past by a free economy that included a built-in system for using that wealth to solve social needs without total dependence on government coercion (see Chapter 4). To restore the system in the modern context, businessmen must exercise their trusteeship of the independent sector with imagination and drive comparable to that which they use in business.

Will they? The evidence begins to suggest that they will. By a general instinct, businessmen have recently begun in very different ways to show a new confidence in their capacity to do what is now most needed by the entire society: to compete effectively with government in broad areas of social service. They have begun to throw off the Depression-bred sense of inadequacy in the face of government bids for public confidence. A few have even discovered that they have decisive advantages over federal techniques as well as pent-up resources for action. The clearest statement I have found came from Federated Stores President Ralph Lazarus this year in his independent sector role as president of United Community Funds and Councils of America:

There are certain social programs, such as unemployment and old-age insurance, that are administratively feasible to approach on a national basis. But not so the major problems that plague us today. Almost all of them are susceptible only to local diagnosis and solution by concerned local citizens. . . .

Government at any level is likely to be slow, unimaginative and too rigid to cope with the speed of social change that now confronts us. It is also too hamstrung by its political commitments to be able to tolerate much of the kind of medicine we need a lot of —creative experimentation in the social field.

Just as important to me is that every time we delegate another job to government—city, state or national—we put one more brick up on the wall of privacy that is shutting us off from concern for our neighbor and his concern for us. Every time a citizen group takes on such a job, it is doing its part to reverse this process.

Going far beyond mere fund-raising, specific industries have begun to act upon problems for which they have a special competence. The banking industry, encouraged by its success in providing low-cost student credit, is hunting other opportunities. Urging them on, Willard C. Rappleye, able editor of the daily *American Banker*, pointed out the special position of leadership held by bankers. "Their unique involvement in the affairs of their communities, their wide dispersal throughout the nation," Rappleye wrote, "place them in a remarkable position to help shape the development of the independent sector."

The industry has begun to respond. Its leaders hope to equip banks as centers of sound financial information on college costs and how to pay them. Bankers have begun to study the whole new category of "self-improvement" loans. As skill requirements change rapidly, more and more people may need continuing re-education. They may need new forms of credit to help them in continuous self-improvement. A group of bankers have worked out and are seeking charters for two private organizations, one to guarantee mortgages, another to provide a secondary market for such mortgages. They aren't asking for federal help. They just want permission to do this job themselves. Even now, only 15 per cent of new mortgage money is FHA-guaranteed.

I expect to see the banking industry move in other and bolder directions. In this era of fast-changing technology, the banking industry may be able to revive the dying breed of young entrepreneurs. To take on more unknown risks, and improve the tools for estimating the character of would-be innovators, banks may need to develop other re-insurance pools.

The self-reform movement may go further. Julius (Jay) Stern, chairman of the Wood County Bank of Parkersburg, West Virginia, has proposed to "examine the present condition of banking in the country, looking toward a resumption of the responsibility for self-regulation which so largely passed out of its hands in the 1930s . . . even the best possible governmental regulation and supervision cannot do our job for us."

In another part of the money trade, an exciting new prospect is on the horizon. Many economic thinkers have long searched for ways to bring about a wider distribution of common stocks. Widespread stock ownership, rather than government redistribution of wealth, is capitalism's best instrument for the creation of a society in which more and more people have the option of leisure or giving their time voluntarily to public service. A few imaginative experts have begun to study independent devices to trigger a much broader base of shareholding.

Time and again lately, far-sighted industries have gone well beyond their conventional role. Insurance companies have banded together to provide low-cost health insurance for older people. It doesn't pay, so it is public business. But more and more insurance companies are doing it. Why? Among the best of reasons is their recognition that whether they like it or not, they are in competition with government for a major area of public service—and public confidence. If they can stick it out, their superior performance may, in the new political climate, show up the failures of the government sector.

So it goes in other industries. In 1960, more than 100 lumber companies operated 303 parks. Private companies owned 53 million acres of timberland, compared to 15.5 million acres of national and state parks, which 50 million people crowded into in 1960. The present expansion of public parks will be more than matched, I suspect, by expansion of privately owned recreation facilities.

Business spends $6–$10 billion annually for training and education. The value of on-the-job training accumulated by all men now in the labor force is estimated at $450 billion.

We've cited other examples in previous chapters: West Virginia Pulp and Paper's anti-pollution efforts, the CED's remarkable effort in planning the economy's reconversion after the war (Chapter 17), the banking industry's exciting response to the credit needs of needy college students. We've seen how multibillion-dollar private urban-renewal efforts dwarf the halting federal renewal scheme.

In 1959, under a headline "Technology and Independent Action under the Free Enterprise System," Curtiss-Wright announced a program of co-operative research and development with industry in other countries in areas normally thought to need government subsidy.

Other companies, big and small, have sensed that one service-rendering commercial plant in a poor nation is a better witness to our system than hours of Voice of America. In Madison, Wisconsin, a brilliant builder named Marshall Erdman decided that he had made enough of a personal fortune but would like to do "something more." He began building at-cost schools in Africa for the Peace Corps. Then, in Tunisia, he saw the primitive, unstandardized building system that requires a highly skilled craftsman to hand-build each part of a house. He recruited a determined Peace Corps veteran to study his Madison company, and go back and set up a business of his own on Erdman capital. Already a bright contrast to Tunisia's primitive socialism, the new company, Erdman believes, proves what other small and medium-size U.S. companies can do on the "big brother" plan. Peace Corps administrators are excited by the idea. So is the Young Presidents' Organization, a trade association of successful young chief executives in America, which has begun to canvass its membership for other big brothers.

Farm organizations are launching bold new programs to strengthen co-operative marketing arrangements as an alternative to federal crop controls and price supports. Experiments are under way with minor farm products— Massachusetts chickens, Kansas lambs, Michigan apples, South Carolina soybeans. Farm leaders hope this experience will show them how to tackle big-volume crops. "If we are going to get the government out," says Charles B. Shuman, president of the vast American Farm Bureau Federation, "we've got to have something to substitute."

The medical profession is rapidly beefing up its once important drug-evaluation program to compete with the U.S. Food and Drug Administration's present near monopoly on drug regulation. The American Medical Association has launched a splendid program of loan guarantees to medical students, has a large and growing program for accrediting nursing homes, and is moving in a dozen ways to act on problems rather than merely criticizing federal proposals.

Employment agencies, galvanized by the government's

stated ambition to monopolize manpower placement, are looking carefully for ways to extend placement services to the hard-core unemployed.

These programs are a mere prelude to the wave of the future. I believe business will soon apply the problem-solving approach systematically and comprehensively. A few months ago I spent several hours with a reporter who had heard we were trying to develop competition with government. He'd torn out the pages of the telephone book which listed all the federal agencies with offices in San Francisco. He asked me to go down the list and spell out independent alternatives to the work of each federal office. I was sore at first, thinking he was trying to make me ridiculous. But why not? A permanent search for alternatives to every government function, present or future, is an urgent and essential task. Business-related research organizations have the ability to do this work. Emerging business leadership will, I believe, prod them into using it. The customer, the public, can only benefit.

I expect to see businessmen take the lead in transferring government enterprises to one of the other two sectors. Commerce can process and deliver millions of quarts of fresh milk to millions of doorsteps every day at dawn, but in many places it cannot, apparently, collect the garbage once a week. For years, government has been nosing into competition with established industries. We may soon see the tables turned, as commercial and independent organizations go after work that government has done poorly.

I expect to see corporations spend their charitable resources much more responsibly. They give to charity now because "they gave last year" or because a powerful customer insists they do. Business has the talent to develop a sounder calculus for charitable investment—indices of need, standards of performance.

To lead the way, businessmen will have to invest their

own time more responsibly than they have in the past. They will learn to refuse tin-cup assignments, choosing instead to solve the independent sector's thorny organizational problems. In this way, they will mobilize other citizens into the proud ranks of the unpaid public servants.

14

The Giant
Stirs

We saw in Chapter 8 how crudely independent institutions often operate, how often they use their energy carelessly, how often they arrange their resources oddly.

But a fresh wind is blowing among these groups. All across the country, independent institutions are getting more self-conscious, aware of, and embarrassed about, their eccentricities. And the beginnings of reform are popping up everywhere—in hospitals, schools, and colleges, community funds, counseling agencies, Boy Scouts, Girl Scouts, and the rest. The number of community symphonies has doubled in a decade and the educational TV net even educates the commercial stations on how to sprinkle a little water on its wasteland programing.

Of course these efforts are often incomplete or misguided, but everywhere you look a new determination has begun to break through.

Take the problem of trusteeship. Any formally organized welfare agency, whether it's a 4-H Club camp or a mental health clinic, has to have a board of trustees or directors, or some equivalent, who presumably are ultimately responsible for the institutions they govern, for the integrity of the operation. They are the stewards of the money and sweat that individual citizens put into the colleges, churches, and welfare agencies they choose to help. These trustees are supposed to set policy and police the managers. Management, presumably, either works well or gets fired.

This is nice, but over the years it has become meaningless. The idea that laymen really control independent organizations has too often been turned into a myth. Boards usually just raise money and vote "yes" on whatever the professional managers want to do.

The trustees of such groups are passive. The initiative usually runs the wrong way. A candid family agency executive says: "We tell them [the board members] how to vote and they vote and we call that process 'the Board sets the policies of the Agency.'"

"Policy formation in the social welfare field . . . is seen as a special contribution of the social work profession," says *The Social Work Yearbook*. Trustees have usually begged money to do whatever the professionals wanted to do. "Trustees," says one observer of hospital trustees, "find themselves relegated to . . . getting the money to pay for whatever the medical board wants."

"One of the greatest wastes of human resources I know is boards of trustees," wrote Milburn "Pete" Akers, as editor of the *Chicago Sun-Times*. They have, he said, "one purpose: ratify that which has been done for the past six months, give them [the administration] a blank check for what they want to do for the next six months."

The people counted on to watch over the independent sector have often secretly abdicated; they just didn't leave their seats. But today as their awareness of their failures grows, a strong counter trend is developing. Two foundations are financing efforts to help college trustees improve their performance (see Chapter 16). We've seen the American Medical Association move boldly into the business of accrediting nursing homes, an important aid to the trustees of nonprofit ones. The U.S. Chamber of Commerce is considering a program of education and research for their many members who are trustees of one or more service institutions.

It is an urgent and universal problem. For example, I have a friend who sits on the board of an agency that counsels people who have family problems. The workers employed by the agency see twenty-two "clients" each week. My friend, who knows that psychiatrists in private practice normally see forty to forty-five patients a week, asks why production runs so low. He's told that heavier loads would ruin the quality of the work. Then he's stuck. He can't find out whether they would or they wouldn't. If he were a part of a national group of trustees, they could study the problem and set up some yardsticks. They could give my friend a standard he could raise and defend, a way to exercise his trusteeship. Now he can't.

We need centralized know-how so we can exercise local responsibility with greater wisdom. The pilot efforts now under way are apt to expand into strong national associations of the trustees of colleges, hospitals, and welfare agencies, set up independently of career administrators and staffed by people who will do solid research and analysis to help trustees do their work.

The air of reform can be felt in other areas. There is growing attention to sound internal management, countering the sorry record of the past.

As we've seen, many service outfits have become almost comically inefficient. Why? Desperately needing the discipline of competition, they have given up competing with government and have outlawed competition among themselves.

These institutions have seen that they face ever greater needs and never have enough money, but they haven't properly used the money they have. They haven't adapted. "Once established, an agency generally continues indefinitely," says the *ad hoc* commission which studied private welfare agencies. Most service organizations have been adrift, puzzled about their role. The country has ceased to expect much from them.

Business holds costs down because it has to. Every business faces every day a conflict between the desire to spend money and the need to save it. Every specialist in every business wants more money in the budget. The sales manager wants more salesmen. The research department wants more researchers. The production department wants better machines. Managers are in the middle. They must decide what the business really needs and what it doesn't.

But almost nobody has managed non-commercial groups this way. Though they have generally been more efficient than government bureaus—for instance, Chicago Youth Centers provide day care for children of working mothers 25 per cent cheaper than most government centers—too few have been under pressure to save money while getting better results.

The technician has wanted to ply his specialty—be it research, social casework, education. He doesn't like to worry about money; saving money gives him a headache. He is an ends-conscious person, fond of a climate where money is no object and waste is justified by good intention. He tends to share, if allowed to, the attitudes of the government professional. "We are not in the business of saving the taxpayer's money," said one such technician. "Our basic identification is with the client and not the taxpayer." Several years ago, Governor Underwood of West Virginia asked some vocational education experts if they wanted the states to take over vocational education from the federal government. They opposed the idea, not in principle, but because "they would be forced into competition with many other demands made at each session of the legislature." So it is with the non-government professionals. Like anybody else, given a choice they would just as soon not have to prove the value of their work.

Worst of all, because the independent sector has often performed so badly, the professionals who run it have been losing their confidence in it and their loyalty to it. They want to get a job done. The independent sector has seemed to fall short. So they have turned more and more to government for help.

Professionals go to government because, as Willy Sutton said of banks, "that's where the money is." Professionals have cared little where their money came from, as long as there was "enough" of it. "The critical issue," says the Problems and Policies Committee of the American Council on Education, "is not how many dollars come from private sources and how many from public sources, but whether or not the total of these dollars will be sufficient to meet the challenges colleges and universities face."

A surveyor talked to professionals in voluntary agencies. Only 20 per cent thought it made any difference whether what they did was paid for by taxes or voluntary gifts. Fifty-seven per cent thought voluntary agencies were doing things government could do better. "What are the strengths of public agencies?" they were asked. "Tax support," said 82 per cent. "What are the weaknesses of voluntary agencies?" "Financing difficulties," said 78 per cent.

So the professionals who run the sector have run it badly and turned to its government competitor for help. They make no bones about it. "Earnest recreationists," says University of Oregon's James Charlesworth, "should exert pressure on every American state legislature to establish a department of recreation." Urging federal aid for social science research, Pennsylvania's Dean Harry Alpert charges his colleagues to "teach as if every student in your class is a potential legislator who will one day have to vote on an appropriation" for what you teach.

But in this area, as in the area of trusteeship, awareness

is growing and reform is afoot. Management consultant firms are being used more and more extensively to find ways to provide "better products for less money." The Ford Foundation has spent millions to turn up ways to administer colleges more responsibly. Acceptance is sometimes painfully slow, but the new effort has reversed three decades of drift. In 1965, Converse College held a conference on the year-round operation of colleges and universities. Compelling data argued for wider acceptance of this money-saving method.

Here and there one even sees a reaction to the crowded crusade for federal funds. The Temporary Woodlawn Organization, a citizen group on Chicago's blighted South Side, turned down federal poverty money. Organizer Saul Alinsky had asked TWO officers to consider carefully whether their full independence might not be a more valuable weapon in their war on slum conditions than federal cash with its inevitable strings. The group did think it over, and decided to go it alone.

Other institutions are finding that federal programs designed to benefit them are new headaches in a green disguise. The colleges that used conventional sources of loans for construction, in preference to "low-cost" federal loans, often saved a lot of money and sleep, in spite of the much lower interest rate for federal construction loans. So more and more private agencies are wondering, rediscovering their competitive relationship, and acting on it.

Givers, I believe, are waking up too. They have drifted into the habit of giving money to institutions carelessly and irresponsibly. We often help independent institutions more out of habit than because we think they are doing work that has to be done. Interviewers asked big givers in a Western city why they give to the charities they do. "Because," most of them said, "we gave last year." But to aid an incompetent organization is to deny aid to competent ones.

We pay the bills of many institutions by co-operative community campaigns. These relieve the giver of "the burden of choice" and keep fund-raisers out of his hair. "Householders are promised liberation from the nuisance of having their doorbells rung," says Richard Carter in *Good Housekeeping* (November, 1959). Central committees divide the money, but the process has often been more political than sensible. "Can any committee—private or governmental—be trusted to decide which cause is worthier?" asks Basil O'Connor of The National Foundation. As you sense the importance of strong service organizations, you find the choice more a pleasure than a burden.

Investing money in the commercial sector is a big business. Investment analysts (7,475 of them) keep track of hundreds of thousands of places in which to put money to work. They watch changes in what customers buy and in the ways companies are run. Investors put dollars where they think they will make the most money. And they get a lot of help. The press reports commercial events in rich detail. Tip sheets by the hundreds tell us about new processes, management changes, new places to put our dollars. Tickers instantly flash information on capital markets across the land. Hundreds of papers quote the value of thousands of stocks every day. The New York Stock Exchange computerizes itself.

We run into many more hazards when we try to invest our money sensibly in nonprofit undertakings. But we have less help on how to make nonprofit dollars pay off. Business givers have paid more attention to what their competitors give to a cause than to its merits. Fund-raising has often been a confidence game. We have given money to causes which sound good. The press, convinced that non-government effort is quaint or sentimental, has rarely bothered to expose waste and self-serving corruption in foundations. When "too many" agencies began to compete for our money, we cheerfully delegated our choices to people who didn't know much more than we did. United giving didn't solve this problem; it just buried it.

But this year, the contributions executives of many of America's top corporations will meet in Quebec to discuss, among other things, how they can invest corporate charitable dollars more sensibly. This is only a beginning. I can see a time when "investors" in independent enterprises will use aids as precise and abundant as those now available to business investors. I can imagine a time when the press will report what the independent sector is doing and what it plans to do, in the same rich detail it now gives to government and commerce.

Another wave of the future is the awareness that independent institutions have too often resisted the commercialization of their activities. Why? Because of a fashionable superstitition which Arthur Miller, the playwright, once stated as a personal dogma: "When a thing becomes commercial, it becomes the enemy of man." This is backward. As a nation grows richer, services which the independent sector once had to supply can be supplied commercially. As their incomes rise, people can pay for more of the services they need. Independent groups should be eager to pass responsibility to the commercial sector and to put their own activities on a business basis. People don't resist paying for things they need. Yet we keep wasting money on services the users should pay for. Independent groups now fight to governmentalize their work; they should look for ways to commercialize it. They've been pushing responsibility the wrong way. The most dedicated liberal would know, if he bothered to consider, that any burden efficiently accepted by commerce is a net gain for the society.

"Everybody benefits—everybody gives," we say to raise money for charity. But the slogan makes more sense for a grocery store or a gas station. If it's true, it means we're not dealing with public problems at all. We've been providing conveniences that users are able and willing to pay for.

We pay to go to the movies, but not the zoo. We pay for our children's bicycles, but not for their full share of the cost of the Boy Scouts. Our college students pay for acres of cars, but not the full cost of tuition or even, in most cases, the cost of university parking lots.

In *The Western Political Quarterly* (December, 1959), Arthur N. Lorig of the University of Washington writes:

> More and more the United Funds are undertaking to foster leisure time activities. Instead of impressing upon youth the importance of self-reliance and self-completeness and individualism, the effect of fund-financed activities would seem to be to teach the youngsters dependency upon contributions from others. Parents, being relieved of some direct responsibility for guiding their children in their leisure time and for paying their expenses, are subjected to this same paternalistic philosophy.

Independent groups have wasted money passing out middle-class welfare in the name of charity. When they do, they are not relieving misery—only inconvenience. But now they are beginning to free themselves to act on the real public problems by charging for services wherever the user can pay for them. Recreation and character-building agencies are leading the way. And the self-help principle can be put to work more fully in education, in family counseling, in cultural activities, in urban renewal, in hospital administration, and in many other fields.

The independent sector is not retreating from its mission as it moves in this direction. It is fulfilling its mission. We should rejoice in the affluence that permits people to pay for services others once had to provide for them. It enables us to use non-commercial resources in new, imaginative ways to solve problems like poverty instead of nursing them.

We can't afford to waste money on activities which can support themselves. We have other urgent work to do.

This movement is spreading. Dean Benjamin Rogge of Wabash College and others have written extensively about the soundness of charging full-cost tuition at college and universities. Meetings of Family Service Associations devote more and more time to discussions of how to depend more on fee income. Hospitals are concerned about realistic pricing. At all levels of government, as well as in the independent sector, fees are being rediscovered as the best way to pay for parks and other city services of all kinds, and their use radically expanded.

Most important, the independent sector is becoming aware of how poorly it uses people and is moving to end this waste of talent. We saw in Chapter 12 how miserably we've failed to design and assign tasks to millions of citizens eager to help. People are getting to work on it. Henry Graham of the Indianapolis Family Service Association has told me excitedly about his promising experiments using non-professionals as assistants. They can often establish contact with troubled families on a more personal basis than the professionals.

A group of us in California are forming the Benjamin Franklin Society, named for the early American who invented, as well as stoves and lightning rods, many independent institutions. Men will pledge to give 5 per cent of their income and to serve five hours a week in independent institutions. But a third condition is more important. Each member will agree to spend those resources of money and time boldly, but thoughtfully, helped in his decisions by other members.

So, in a thousand ways, we now see the third sector straining against its backward forms and occasionally breaking through with surges of energy and imagination. It looks like a ship which is tacking its way slowly out of the harbor but will soon go under full sail.

15

The Churches:
Centers of Concern

My father preached in a Presbyterian church in Indiana. The church was run by a group of "ruling elders." Another group, the deacons, did what they could for the poor people in the parish. They handled what we called the deacon's fund, paying out money for groceries, coal, or shoes. During the Depression, business was brisk. The deacons met in our parlor once a week for soul-testing decisions on how they could use their pitiful little fund to help relieve the mountain of human distress in our town.

The deacon business soon changed. As the church gave up its welfare effort to government, the deacons slowly retreated into ceremony. They met less and less often because they had nothing to do. Today, to justify their titles, they usher people to their seats on Sunday and pass the collection plates. If a dog wanders into the narthex during the service, they chase it out. The very word deacon has, tragically, become comical.

Perhaps you heard of the preacher who misread the lines of a mighty hymn about the church's strength and sang lustily from the pulpit: ". . . Her task *un*equal to her strength. . . ." It was a Freudian slip, for it spoke a hidden truth. The church has real strength to help troubled people, and Christ's life told Christians to dare, to sacrifice, to use their strength to the limit in the service of others. But the church in America has given up the ghost, quit using its strength. Reporter Harrison Salisbury wrote, in his prize-winning articles on New York's juvenile gangs:

> Churches tend to cater to their own congregations and with rare exceptions are reluctant to assume responsibility for the whole community in which they are situated or for any deprived areas elsewhere.

Some churches have done better than others. The Mormons have never given up meeting the real needs of all their fellow members. Jewish groups have pioneered new solutions to such ever changing problems as the agony of our elders; individual Jewish businessmen often do more than their share in secular agencies. Catholic churches have remained, as a rule, more active than their Protestant counterparts, especially in the big cities. Special-purpose religious groups, like the Salvation Army, still beat the drums even though their organization and techniques have often become archaic. The Mission Doll in the Broadway musical *Guys and Dolls* reminded us of something joyful we had lost.

As the church, pushed aside by government, gave up its serious social business, most of its welfare leaders found ways to rationalize the situation. "The churches and their social welfare agencies should promote the adoption of legislation to improve public health and welfare," declared the National Council of Churches' National Conference on Policy and Strategy in Social Welfare at its Atlantic City convention in 1957. By 1961, some Protestant leaders were officially washing their hands of direct responsibility. The National Council's Conference on Social Welfare sent this statement to the member denominations "for study":

The provision for social welfare is the responsibility of the total community functioning through the channels of government.

The consequences soon became obvious. To be a church member became easy and automatic, an extra value accepted like Green Stamps. Something was missing. The postwar surge in membership represented, some ministers sensed, an earnest search for personal meaning. But the new members were offered a cup of coffee rather than a demand upon conscience. The church was rendering unto Caesar its job of concern with people. Earnest ministers, persuaded that only government could be an instrument of public service, turned to highly political arguments for federal legislation. The Good Samaritan story was edited a bit: he became the man who would vote to give other people's money to anybody left hurt along the wayside.

"We Christianized the federal government because we wouldn't tithe to do the job ourselves," insists Granville Clark, a responsible small-town lawyer in Kentucky. As the welfare programs spread, they had a curiously dehumanizing effect upon all of us. "The average American today has no twinge of conscience when he passes the sick man on the road," says a veteran welfare worker. "He knows he has paid the Good Samaritan to come along after him and take care of this rather unpleasant social obligation." The irony of this attitude is grasped by Negro intellectuals, who use "white liberal" to damn a man who talks generously but acts miserly with his time and friendship.

The average layman at church is left with an incomplete religious experience. By abdication of its concern for others, by deliberate delegation of its Good Samaritan power, the church in effect leads members into the sin of self-concern. The layman is invited to use the church for self-improvement instead of service. Of course, the churches still say, "Love thy neighbor . . ." but church practice is more persuasive than its preaching. The layman is denied the direct witness of love for his fellow man, by which he would learn, the ministers tell us, to love God. Shut off from personal involvements with those in trouble, he can no longer "make a difference" by his action. So he has little church experience that will help him believe he makes any difference to God.

Small wonder the layman feels obsolete, puzzled, angry. He is left to wonder why he goes to church. Is it to take cold comfort in the church's bad example?

Worried observers charge that the church is growing listless. While more members go into the pews, less energy comes out. The subtraction of service from the church's mission, more than any theological crisis, has caused her lethargy. The former head of the National Conference of Catholic Charities said, "When the proponents of the new public welfare reach their utopia, there will no longer be a place for religion in the American community."

The church's acceptance of an insignificant role in American society has alarming consequences outside the church. For one thing, we have turned off a mighty source of energy. Almost 118 million people in 320,000 congregations are told there is nothing special for them to do but be pious and pay their taxes. This is, if nothing worse, a shocking waste of human resources.

Let's put the waste up against one urgent domestic problem, hard-core unemployment. Something less than a million people make up the "unemployable" cases—about three per church—and recent research indicates that almost every human talent can be developed. If the average church helped three people out of helpless poverty into productive employment, the formidable problem would come tumbling down like the walls of Jericho. Hard-core unemployment won't be solved just this way, of course, though some churches have begun again to try. The figures simply illustrate how small our big problems can look when laid alongside the church's idle plant and talent.

The church's withdrawal from service cannot, I believe, be more than temporary. The central thrust of Christianity has been its ultimate involvement with mankind. As the ministers and laymen sense the emptiness of a mission which excludes human service, they will move to revive their responsibility. As the churches see the dehumanizing consequences of government welfare monopoly, they will have no choice.

The signs of a new direction have already begun to appear. Even while the church has been generally receding from responsibility, specific events have been hinting that we were not far from the lowest tide. In the fifties, restless laymen, both Protestant and Catholic, began to assert their sense of new purpose even against clergy resistance. The Christian Family Movement, founded not by a priest but by lawyer Patrick Crowley and his wife, sprang up in the Midwest and spread all over the world. An activist movement, CFM became the fastest growing new element in Roman Catholicism. The University of San Francisco prepared to train Catholicism's first "lay theologians"—married men who had succeeded in the secular world but wanted to function in priest-like vocations. They became strong new workers, as did Catholicism's first lay missionaries. The priests themselves began to search for new responsibility. The late Samuel Cardinal Stritch sent Monsignor John Egan, a ball of organizing fire, into Chicago's teeming South Side to work out a church program for the rising urban crisis.

Individuals produced dramatic examples of how the church need not stand aside for government in welfare work. In Detroit's Corktown, Father Clement H. Kern painted his church bright white. "The people hear that there's a big white place where they can get help," he said, and he helped immigrant Mexicans and Negroes with services ranging from a foot clinic to a job-finding agency.

The ferment in Catholicism revived significant elements of the church's rich social doctrine. In a sense, these doctrines describe the function of America's independent sector, define its independence from government and its contribution to personal freedom. Drawing on this literature, the Catholic bishops of the United States issued a stirring message in 1960:

> The history of the achievements of America stands as a monument to the personal responsibility of free men. If our future is to be worthy of our past, if the fruit of America's promise is not to wither before it has reached full maturity, our present preëminent need is to reaffirm the sense of individual obligation, to place clearly before ourselves the foundation on which personal responsibility rests, to determine the causes of its decay and to seek the means by which it can be revived.
>
> A fresh evocation of the principle and practice of personal responsibility can revivify our society and help to stem the seemingly inexorable march toward the automation of human beings and the steady loss of that freedom which is man's distinctive attribute. It will stimulate a self-reliance which will automatically restore the balance between freedom and security.

In Protestantism, the same kind of thing began to happen, perhaps in greater variety. A racketeer-turned-preacher, Jim Vaus, set up an electronics school in East Harlem's worst precinct for juvenile crime, offered the salvation of both technology and religion to a carefully selected clientele of street-gang leaders. The local crime rate dropped sharply, and the businessmen backing Vaus invested in a summer camp for other slum victims. On college campuses around the country, chaplains often organized the new battalions of students going into slums to teach dropouts. This nation-wide program would have been laughed off campus only a few years ago in the panty-raid era.

The church was dragged backward into the racial crisis. Had the whole independent sector, including the churches, been in a vital condition, this job would never have been left to the crude, often cruel, instruments of government. The harsh, bloody encounters between federal and state politicians need never have taken place—and did not, even in crisis, whenever citizen leadership held its own (see Chapter 17). As the churches gradually began to confront the bitter issue, the majority of ministers first showed a greater interest in the difficulties of distant communities than in the injustice of their own parish. Some preached for legislation—to self-satisfied Northerners in white-only parishes. But as time goes by and political action reaches its natural limit, the churches must turn to the permanent helping programs in literacy, housing, employment—and even in their segregated witness at eleven o'clock each Sunday morning. Unless the flexible, infinitely complex machinery of the independent sector is fully engaged, preaching on racial justice will never be much more than a political demand for the "civil rights" that government can grant. On the other hand, we may see startling developments. If the churches really try to educate the deprived, for instance, they may revive the college-building business at which they once excelled.

The churches, with their proper concern for every human regardless of the body he wears, have a special mission to people who have been cast aside. To exercise this concern is to revitalize the church. In the recent surge of such work, many churches around the country have begun to take responsibility for the ever larger numbers of old people.

San Francisco's Council of Churches hired, with foundation help, a wise Jewish mother named Beatrice Schiffman to organize an experimental network of senior centers. An experienced social worker, Bea Schiffman soon proved that weekly doses of loving attention, deftly administered by church volunteers, could work wonders. It could rescue an agonizing elder from anger, despair, and even the symptoms of senile depression. "We must love them," she admonishes her Christian volunteers, "no matter how unattractive they make themselves."

As the church-run centers served old men and women by the hundreds, they also put new life and joy into the host congregations. The ministers of San Francisco's Protestant denominations began to marvel at the result and hunt for explanations. For too long, some decided, the churches have just sat and accepted people who came and acted like proper members of the flock. By reaching out to help embittered old people who have been pushed aside by the rest of the society, the churches suddenly found themselves again doing what churches ought to do. You could feel the change every Sunday.

The point is hard to miss. Our secular society tends to hide the old, the mentally ill, the uneducated, the black, the retarded—to store them out of sight as the government stores surplus grain. With the resources to correct this barbaric practice, the churches seem to be finding the faith to act.

---
*

16

Foundations:
Citizen Risk Capital

---
*

American foundations are big business. They are worth $14.5 billion; they spend more than $750 million a year. The list includes 6,000 foundations of significant size, and 176 with assets exceeding $10 million. But their relative importance, according to foundation expert F. Emerson Andrews, "has sharply declined."

Foundations think of themselves as America's laboratory. They pay for risky research; they experiment; they promote new things; they challenge the status quo. Their strength is their flexibility. They can't seek profit; they don't have to seek public acclaim. They can try damn-fool things. Created by profit from the commercial sector, they provide the distinctive risk capital of the independent sector.

However, they have tended lately to lose sight of their special character. Professor Galbraith called American foundations "essentially arms of the welfare state." He was describing a passing distortion rather than a permanent condition. Foundations, on the whole, don't want to do anything on a permanent basis. They want to keep their resources free for experimentation. Their support, in the idiom of the trade, is usually terminable. Thus, the works they pioneer have to be carried on by other agencies which want permanent responsibility. And this, in recent decades, has been the government.

At first, foundations promoted government action by accident. But now they often do it on purpose. Most foundations have come to think they should help the government expand. So they find unmet human needs. They look for remedies. They run pilot projects. They arouse public opinion. When the time is ripe, they pass responsibility to government.

Leonard Mayo, executive director of the Association for the Aid of Crippled Children, says: "The private foundation can . . . act as an informal 'agent' for a governmental group, arousing interest in and helping to interpret the need for a project that the latter is prepared to support."

John D. Rockefeller III, chairman of the board of the Rockefeller Foundation, said in 1964:

> The fact that private philanthropy has recognized . . .
> basic human needs and has led government to meet
> them is part of the social history of our century. We
> should not resist this trend: rather we should en-
> courage it.

"A classic example of the way philanthropy is supposed to work," writes Robert Bremmer in *American Philanthropy* (University of Chicago Press, 1960), "was when Foundation grants pioneered 'talking books' for the blind. After the foundations had perfected the program, Congress began to appropriate money to the Library of Congress to permit nation-wide extension of the service."

"Private philanthropy very often provides the means whereby an activity can be started on a small scale, with the ultimate result that the activity may be taken over on a larger scale under public auspices once its value has been demonstrated," says a Columbia University economist. The famous Rockefeller Brothers Fund reports all called for more government action.

I worked for a certain foundation for several years. We received hundreds of requests from health, welfare, and education groups every year. Almost all the requests ended the same way. Here is a letter I saved because it is so brief and direct: "Here are some ideas we want money for at the College. We expect the City to take over when we have demonstrated values." We see this spirit everywhere. It is what foundations think they are supposed to do.

This policy is right in one way and wrong in another. Foundations should pioneer, break new ground for others to cultivate. But without quite knowing why, they have been pioneering the wrong frontier. They should, I believe, be pioneering the new frontier of independent action. They should guide other independent agencies into broader responsibility.

The foundations are not, as some conservative critics proclaim, conspiring to socialize America. If General Motors were the only producer of cars, an inventor would have only one place to take automotive inventions. As government has emerged as the only active competitor for public responsibility, it became the principal market for social innovation, the foundation's natural product.

The re-emergence of the independent sector is opening up many new opportunities to foundations. In research, for example, foundations can begin to mine the wealth of information about the submerged independent sector, the very ground on which the foundation stands. We know least about the sector of our society Tocqueville thought most important. We don't know how big the independent sector is, what it does, what it could do. In gathering material for this book, I was astonished at the scarcity of solid information. You see examples of independent action in every newspaper, but the disciplined method of scholarship has not often been applied to this data. Studies which spell out the size and strength of America's independent institutions deserve a high priority.

We need related studies of how responsibility is now shared among the three sectors in America. The whole purpose of our political process is to distribute responsibility among our institutions, yet we don't even know how responsibility is divided. Such studies would, I'm sure, be full of surprises. Few of us realize how much responsibility the independent sector carries in some fields, how little in others. We will not really know America until we know her independent sector. Foundations can give the independent sector the self-awareness it needs to restore its confidence and its determination to build for the future.

This literature has yet to be written. There are a few descriptive studies, an occasional history of an individual philanthropist or foundation or welfare agency. F. Emerson Andrews' Foundation Library Center has been gathering information about some of our independent institutions, but the library's small size is a measure of the job yet to be done. In time, however, this literature can become as rich and extensive as the literature of political economy.

The theoretical literature of the independent sector— books that spell out why independent action works—can greatly accelerate its progress. One or two foundation leaders have begun to look for ways to encourage scholarship in this field. Now and then a writer stumbles onto a fascinating discovery. Jane Jacobs wrote in *The Death and Life of Great American Cities:*

> the public peace of cities is not kept primarily by the police, necessary though they are. It is kept by an intricate, almost unconscious network of voluntary controls and standards among the people themselves. In some city areas . . . the keeping of public sidewalk law and order is left almost entirely to the police and special guards. These areas are jungles.

In short, Mrs. Jacobs glimpsed the invisible hand of responsible action at work in our cities. But nobody followed up her insight with a detailed explanation of how this intricate system operates.

Many natural forces work invisibly in society. Harvard Professor Carle Zimmerman, the distinguished sociologist, discovered another in his pioneering studies of family life. About a generation ago our families seemed to be going to pieces. The faster pace of life, the headlong flight from the farm, the Great Depression, had thrown the American family into a confusing new way of life. Families crowded into strange, lonely cities, lost their balance, and began to break apart in shocking numbers.

The results began to pile up—rocketing rates of crime, school dropouts, swollen welfare rolls. Nothing has added so much to the agenda of public business as the seeming breakdown of American family life. People began to look outside the family for remedies to problems that began at home. The school tried to deal with the "whole" child; social workers tried to stand in for absent or careless parents. We set up a growing array of public agencies to do the work families left undone.

But all the time, the American family has been quietly learning to solve its own new problems. Zimmerman and his associates found that millions of American families are learning how to stabilize themselves. They build a protective wall around their families by carefully building friendships with other families whose values are like their own. It works. These families keep their children in school and out of trouble. Zimmerman had seen the invisible hand at work again. No government planner or university sociologist arranged these families. They did what had to be done themselves, moved by a desperate necessity, and guided by common sense. In the same unconscious way, many of our voluntary institutions have slowly begun an instinctive reformation. But a sharper understanding of the forces at work would help us accelerate purposeful reform.

The 1956 Report of the Princeton Conference on the History of Philanthropy in the United States called for research "comparing the relative effectiveness of America's distinctive voluntary pattern with that of countries where the state assumes responsibility. There appears to be some evidence that action is taken sooner and sometimes more effectively under voluntary auspices, but careful comparative studies would be needed to test this thesis." This is a challenge. But it is also a shocking admission of our ignorance of America's most vital force.

We know little about the service motive. We see evidence that it exists. We sense that nobody wants to be reduced to a social security number, a wage earner who now and then votes. But we need to study more carefully the impulse to selfless service, see what forms it takes and how it can best be fortified and released.

As our understanding of the foundation's function improves, foundation leadership will face many other immediate, practical problems of improving their effectiveness. We've seen repeatedly the need for guides to sensible philanthropic investment. How can we tell a sound charitable organization from an unsound one? How do we establish priorities? We have a head start in this effort. Economists have developed useful "cost-benefit ratios" to evaluate the relative merits of public projects in difficult areas, like water and power development and flood control. We've seen the nearly universal need for aids to trustees of independent institutions. Foundations are already at work. The Carnegie Foundation is financing one newsletter for college trustees. The Relm Foundation of Ann Arbor, Michigan, is paying for the pilot edition of another.

The independent sector needs innovation more than anything else. We need to focus more and more of our fabulous research and development know-how on the problems of independent action. Not long ago I was talking to two brilliant economists at Stanford Research Institute. I was looking for ways to find new productive job opportunities for low-skilled people. These two men were full of fascinating ideas. "Why," I asked them, "haven't you pursued these concepts?" There was, they claimed, no client—no one to pay the cost of research like this. In other words, everybody's business is nobody's business. But foundations have the freedom to sponsor such research and to experiment in bold applications of the results.

This is a unique and natural opportunity for American philanthropy—to finance the speculative search for better independent methods of doing things. We have an inventory of sticky public problems: rocketing hospital costs, gross inefficiency in higher education, the prohibitive cost of psychiatric treatment, the need for imaginative voluntary methods of assembling land for urban redevelopment, and a host of others. Most needed are careful studies of how we can mobilize people to solve public problems, to answer the question "What Can I Do?" with precision and comprehension.

And foundations are the natural underwriters of speculative new independent enterprises. A foundation paid the bills of the United Student Aid Funds program (Chapter 11) until it was clear it would work. Carnegie's founding interest in Teachers Insurance and Annuity Association (Chapter 6) is a classic example of innovative philanthropy.

In this field, foundations can well imitate the methods of the commercial investment firms that deliberately seek out high-risk ventures and form bold, effective partnerships with creative enterprisers. It is a common complaint that we have too many independent agencies. Perhaps we do, but because too few die and not because too many are born. It is harder than it should be to start new enterprises in this sector, though they are often the best. Too much wealth is poured into safe but tired established agencies, too little channeled to new-idea men who could brighten and invigorate the independent sector.

The true development of the foundation will come when it accepts the discipline of competition with government and thus is forced to bold innovation. Without this function, the foundation gives up its unique role and the only one that is politically defensible.

This competitive task takes on new urgency as the government moves relentlessly to finish off its already battered competitors. The independent sector will be cut back further, perhaps abolished, if it fails to compete aggressively in public service.

In eighteenth-century France, the government in fact outlawed independent action. Shelby McCloy told the grim story in *Government Assistance in Eighteenth-Century France* (Duke University Press, 1946):

> Throughout the century there was a steady shift of burden from private and church charities to state charities, from local to provincial and governmental assistance. . . . The change resulted from the repeated failure of church, private and municipal charities to meet the situation, the state being forced to intervene with its aid, in response to piteous appeals. This tendency grew so rapidly in the second half of the century that prior to the Revolution the opinion had come to be rather general that care of its needy subjects was a state obligation. . . . The revolutionary governments moved by rapid strides toward the full realization of this ideal. All endowments and other revenues of eleemosynary institutions were suppressed or confiscated by the government; church property was seized and church moneys for charities disap-

peared; even the philanthropic societies were abolished. . . .

Already in America, government is tightening its grip on the independent sector. It is challenging the tax-exempt status of foundations, making new efforts to "regulate" almost all private groups. An independent sector "regulated" by its competition has, at best, an uphill fight on its hands.

Without a sure sense of what they should do, foundations themselves have become more and more vulnerable to this political attack. The government is eyeing foundation treasuries hungrily. Every year the pressures mount for their closer government control. Congressional committees regularly badger them. Congressman Wright Patman of Texas has proposed a new agency to regulate them. The treasury has just suggested elaborate new restrictions. But this movement couldn't flourish if the foundations pursued their natural mission efficiently and relentlessly.

The logic of the foundation-busters is formidable. Foundations, they argue, have money because they don't pay taxes. So, it is said, they are really spending tax money. Officials elected by all the people should control tax money, this argument says, not foundation trustees who elect each other.

But this assault will collapse as foundations find an essential job which the government by nature can't do. Justice Horace Gray of the Massachusetts Supreme Court set forth a still standard legal definition of charity in 1867— to "lessen the burdens of government."

This definition is all right as far as it goes. But the foundation is more than a mechanical alternative to government action—and far more than an arm of the welfare state suitable only to test out and lobby for new federal programs. The foundation is an instrument forged by citizens who transfer profit from the commercial sector and put it directly to work as risk capital for the general betterment of the society. To say or imply that the foundation exists only on the sufferance of government is to reason from the premise that government is the whole society. Here is a special version of the untenable notion that the citizen and all his institutions are creatures of the state, not the other way around. The government has no natural "burden," no divine franchise on public responsibility. It simply does the chores we leave for it to do.

Such language seems awkward in a society accustomed to think of responsibility as something that should be promptly bundled off to Washington, not proudly borne at home. But the right to take social responsibility is an essential part of the human enterprise, and the private foundation an essential resource. It is a distinctive means to build a society in which each individual serves to the limit of his ability and concern.

17

Chief Citizens
in Politics

Not long ago, shortly after *Look* published an article about the emerging independent sector and some of my ideas about it (December 29, 1964), Governor George Romney summoned George Harris, who wrote the *Look* piece, and me to Lansing. We found, when we arrived, that he had gathered his staff for the occasion. We spent a long winter's afternoon talking about what he, as Governor, could do in Michigan to encourage the independent sector.

I was perfectly certain of the sincerity of the Governor's interest. He is one of the first American political figures to feel the urgency of an independent revival. He speaks about it with an eloquence and conviction that could not be put on. When he opened the poverty program's first center in Detroit, he made a hopeful point. "This is not only a place for people to come who need help," he said, "it is also a place for people to come who want to help."

But what could he do, as Governor, to assist the independent sector without subverting its independence? It was a problem I had never faced squarely before, and I found it fascinating. We all left Lansing with more questions than we had come with and fewer answers. What should a governor do to assist his independent competitor?

We will get answers only when we begin to think realistically about how public policy gets formed. We looked at this briefly in Chapter 10. We have some very strange ideas about the legislative process. We speak of it as if we send to legislatures wise men who think up policies and put them into law. We tend to see our legislators operating like scoutmasters assigning camp chores: Charley to cook the hash, Eddie to do the dishes, and George to dig the garbage hole. We speak of "policy-making" as if policy were something that is willfully formed.

But government policy is not made by politicians. Policy *emerges*, as a result of the action of people and institutions in the society. The Congressman's vote is a specialized and limited tool. Voting stamps a specific piece of public policy, after the basic structure has been built. As we have seen, policy is the complex, mixed, often contradictory result of a competition for public responsibility. Congress is the judge of the race, but the race itself is much more important than the judging. The outcome depends more on how the race is run than upon the formal designation of the winner. The independent sector—like the commercial sector— loses responsibility when it runs badly, or it stands and argues that there is no race.

From this point of view, we can begin to sort out the roles of the various parties acting in the process. The permanent bureaucracy's role is clear. They are in the race. (It's tempting but vain to moralize about whether they should or should not be. They just are.) The role of the emerging independent sector's leaders is clear. They should seek responsibility, they too should be in the race.

Elected officials, from Congressmen at the national level down to city councilmen, are the judges, even though partisan. We send them because we respect their judgment, because we believe their values would lead them to judge evidence much as we would. When we think, as we often do now, of government as the only instrument of social action, we favor the politician who talks only of government action. He gains an advantage from our ignorance.

But what about the chief executive officers? We elect them, as we do our Congressmen. They become for a time the bosses of the permanent bureaucracies at various levels. Where do they fit? Are they judges of the race, runners, or both?

The question is useful. We have seen how the temporary eclipse of the independent sector has warped the role of Congress. They become the board of trustees of an essentially uncontrollable public service monopoly. I suddenly realized, as we talked to Governor Romney, that the eclipse of independent action had twisted and constricted the role of elected executives in much the same way.

It seems clear to me that the chief executive of any political unit, be he President or governor or mayor, has a special, forgotten relationship to the independent sector. We send one of ourselves, a layman, to the White House or the state house or to city hall, not to become only an administrator of bureaucratic establishments and thus the automatic spokesman for ever bigger government. The President is not in Washington just to run the federal store or to keep an eye on the permanent staff. As our chief citizen, he is also potentially the chief patron of the independent sector.

The President now goes through certain ceremonial motions which survive the day when the independent sector had more vigor. He is the honorary chairman of the Red Cross. He endorses many major national fund-raising campaigns, often kicks off the United Fund drives by an appeal on the TV networks, and now and then he says nice things about private charity.

This chief citizen role of the President got lost in the Depression. The Roosevelt years were years when, with public confidence in the independent sector all but exhausted, Presidential energy was channeled almost wholly into the radical expansion of government. Presidential responsibility to the independent sector, if not overlooked completely, was de-emphasized. There were, of course, exceptions. President Roosevelt, a polio victim, put his formidable prestige behind the independent March of Dimes, which all but wiped out polio.

Equally interesting, if less well known, was the part Secretary of Commerce Jesse Jones played in the formation of the Committee for Economic Development at the end of World War II. Looking ahead during the early years of the war, Jones saw there would be tremendous pressure for government action to ease the pain of transition from wartime to peacetime production. Jones believed the problem to be extravagantly overstated, that independent action would be preferable to the government plans he saw on the drawing boards of the federal bureaucracies. He called in the nation's business leadership, challenged them to meet the need for independent planning of the production transition. Top corporate leaders created the Committee for Economic Development for this specific purpose. A week after V-E Day, amid a chorus of doom-saying prophecy, CED boldly announced its program and confidently forecast a smooth transition. Fifty thousand businessmen acting through two thousand local committees did the postwar planning. The massive transition from wartime to peacetime production was guided by an independent effort, because one man in government knew that he could rely upon resources far greater than those inside government. The independent sector was prodded and encouraged by a member of the Cabinet. So far as I know, no tax money changed hands.

Examples of this sort were rare in the New Deal period. The federal mandate was to build government action without a thought for alternatives. One might have expected a change under Eisenhower, who had won on a "time for a change" campaign that touted decentralization. He wanted to pass responsibility back, if not to the still invisible independent sector, at least to states and cities. "This accelerating pull to the center must be curbed," he said; "the government of every town and city and state must bear local responsibility." He may have thought at first he could unwind government like a ball of twine. In the end, he resignedly toyed with a few loose ends.

He tried to return some minor federal jobs to the states. For example, he wanted the states to take on the job of treating sewage—not poverty or unemployment, just sewage. He wanted to take the federal hand, subsidy and all, out of the disposal business. And he didn't try to push the responsibility back very far—just one notch, to the states, not to the independent sector or even to cities or counties. He didn't even ask that they pay the bills. He offered to give the states a federal tax source, a part of the tax on telephone calls.

Certainly this was a modest proposal. But General Dwight David Eisenhower, who led the armored legions that crushed the Axis powers, could not force the sovereign states to take the responsibility for treating sewage. This campaign he lost.

The states, in effect, told the General to go to hell. They fought the plan. So did the cities. So did the businessmen who sell pumps and sewer pipe. The state health officers? They not only fought the transfer; they wanted to expand the federal program.

Ike kept trying. He wanted the cities to take more responsibility for urban renewal. The American Municipal Association, with thirteen thousand members, denounced him and asked for a bigger federal program. He stood before a meeting of the REA cooperatives and begged them, since they had almost finished their job of electrifying farms, to get off the dole—to become independent. They asked for more federal money than ever.

Eisenhower failed, I think, for a neglected reason. He tried the impossible: to pass responsibility to people who didn't want it. You cannot press responsibility upon anybody unwilling to accept it—not local government, or business, or the independent institutions. Eisenhower, whose lifelong experience had been within government, sought to pass responsibility down toward the local levels of government. He accepted the States' rights doctrine, but did not see that it deals with only one part of our traditional system for diffusing responsibility. He missed, I think, the institutions most likely to accept more work.

In another instance, Ike had better luck with a different approach. He used the independent sector by accident, but never understood its broader dimension. Racial segregation in Washington's movie theaters outraged foreign diplomats. So Ike called the big chain-theater operators to the White House. Though they asked at first for an executive edict to protect them against white anger, they saw the benefit of acting quietly and on their own—but in concert. Presto—no more segregated movies in the nation's capital, no federal edict, no trouble. The change came so smoothly that CORE pickets, who had been trying to buy tickets in integrated groups, suddenly found themselves admitted to dull films they did not really want to see. Some were angry at the sudden end of the controversy.

You would think that such an easy success on a nagging problem would have led Ike to more of the same. The theater owners, acting as a group in the public interest—against what they considered to be their commercial interest—provided a small, clear example of action by the independent sector. In this case, as in others, an *ad hoc* independent group accepted responsibility far more quickly than is the habit of state and local government. Yet the lesson was lost, and federal court orders continued to be the main pattern of integration for some years. President Eisenhower, lacking a clear concept of independent devices, never expanded his accidental success beyond one problem, race, in what had become his home town, Washington.

Oddly enough, the Kennedy Administration quietly ran experiments in the delicate art of depending upon independent groups for decisive, important moves. Perhaps the Kennedy habit of inventing new instruments of power led to the tests, but President Kennedy learned in these instances not to be heavy-handed. As in Ike's case, it was the racial crisis that forced him to search for something better than the blunt instruments of government.

After the Birmingham riot of 1963, one business leader brought the heads of fifty major corporations to the White House. The President explained the danger of Negro violence spreading across the nation, asked for advice and help. The businessmen responded by pointing out ways in which the federal bureaucracy had made it difficult for them to remove racial barriers in some areas. Then, working as a group, the businessmen plotted their independent strategy. By the time of the "jobs and freedom" march on Washington, center of government, Negroes were getting their best new job opportunities out of the major corporations, through organized independent action. Most of the press never caught on to the results of this drive.

Meanwhile, one special group of businessmen operated under the leadership of Julius Manger, Jr., owner of the Manger Hotel chain based in Savannah, Georgia. Like many other Southerners, Manger knew that pickets and government pressure would inspire violence. Whatever he thought of integration, he saw a responsibility to his region and he acted with courage. After ending segregation in his own Deep South hotels, he went to other Southern cities and worked with the operators of chain theaters, motels, restaurants, and dime-store lunch counters. Between May and October of 1963, businessmen acted decisively in 64 per cent of 566 cities, big and small, in the South and border states.

The businessmen and Southerners who did the serious work never wanted publicity. In many Southern communities today, a committee of businessmen and other community leaders, often a secret membership, accepts permanent responsibility for meeting with Negroes and working out solutions to each new problem.

Thus the civil rights movement, as the most dramatic current manifestation of independent action, has achieved some of its most durable successes in levering the commercial sector into action. Surely its greatest frustrations lie in its early overemphasis on government action. The movement's long-term future, I believe, lies in the rediscovery of the growing potential of its natural permanent allies in the independent sector to solve the staggering minority problems which lie beyond civil rights.

Amid the years of headlines about the South, few reporters have caught on to a simple fact: even after federal intervention, serious trouble has erupted only when the independent leadership, mainly businessmen and bankers, has lost control to local politicians.

The racial crisis has provided the most severe test possible of all our institutions in all sectors. Time and again it has demonstrated that responsibility goes only to those willing to take it, often at risk. To an extent far greater than we know, it is the independent sector which has been quietly effective.

However, Governor Romney has run up against a serious problem in Michigan. Eager to pass on responsibility to independent agencies, he has found many that are not as eager to accept it as he is to give it. They have lost the habit. One of his aides told of a painful record. "When we call a conference of the independent agencies in the state," he said, "they come with lists of things they want the state to do." Romney is trying to turn the question around, get them to ask what they can do for their state.

It is clear that if the independent sector is to take a heavier load in America, two conditions must exist together. Our elected representatives, particularly the elected executives, must be receptive to independent solutions. And, on the other side, independent institutions must want to take responsibility. If either condition is absent, the effort must fail. When they occur together, success is certain.

A President or governor has a natural role as patron of the independent sector, and this function needs to be revived. It is a delicate task. To patronize the independent sector in the wrong way will corrupt its independence, in time destroy it. For example, independent institutions cannot long maintain their independence if they live on government money. They are independent precisely because they do not. A great school like M.I.T. can lose its initiative on a diet of fat federal grants. I am scared to death, for example, that the poverty program may stultify some of our finest independent agencies, weigh them down with politics and bureaucracy.

The spirit of the poverty program is good. It is based on the idea that thirty years of government effort has, on the whole, failed to find ways to help the poor escape poverty. We have families who have been on relief for three generations. Those who are succeeding with the poor, helping them climb out of poverty—like the Y.M.C.A., Urban League, community welfare councils—are independent institutions. It seems logical then to subsidize the independent institutions. And, just as logically, that is how to kill them. You can almost see the work slow down and the "co-ordination" begin, the substitutions of administrators for workers. And then the paper blizzard. The tragedy is that the final effect of the poverty program may be to destroy the agencies which could eliminate poverty. The deadening effect of federal finance on our research effort should be warning enough.

When confronted with previous federal expansion, conservatives have misjudged the nature of the immediate danger. They see federal control following federal money. But they have talked about the takeover as if it were a Martian invasion. Federal control does not mean harsh oppression. If schools, for example, become dependent on federal dollars, no storm troopers will march in to rip pages out of the textbooks and intimidate the teachers. The threat of federal dependence is not the iron fist but the soft blanket of conformity that will slowly—worse yet, painlessly—smother initiative, human variety, and innovation.

The idea that the President can help the independent sector only with federal money is nonsense. The independent sector needs money much less than it needs a place in the sun, visibility, recognition, moral support, and, most of all, defense against blind bureaucratic encroachment.

I do not have enough specific answers to satisfy you or me. But here are some possibilities. The President could assist the independent sector in breaking the monopoly of the federal bureaucracy on the ear of Congress. He could become, through his Cabinet, the early warning system that the independent sector so desperately needs, alerting independent leadership to emerging competitive challenges. White House Conferences have degenerated into prearranged endorsements of federal ambitions. They could, I believe, become the means whereby the independent sector's plans and solutions are laid before the nation.

The President could point out opportunities for independent action, put challenges before the people. The Peace Corps moved slightly in that direction. But it blindly ignored a century of dedicated independent effort. I think it could have worked better had the President merely challenged the independent sector—universities and churches as well as business groups—to expand their already substantial efforts. The Peace Corps did not need to be governmental. It is, I believe, strong to the degree that it uses the independent energy of the Corpsmen, weak to the degree that federal finance makes bureaucracy inevitable, later if not in the first flush of excitement. The business-backed *Acción* program in Venezuela shows more long-term promise than does the more rigid Peace Corps.

Elected officials can legitimately assist independent institutions by the expansion of tax incentives. This approach can break the vicious cycle which now artificially limits the resources of the third sector. Government tends to claim that independent resources are inadequate and then makes them more inadequate by high taxes. Every tax dollar is a dollar which might have been available to the independent sector. The government should not be permitted to pre-empt the nation's money and then criticize the consequences. Tax incentives can to some degree restore this balance without, I believe, compromising the independent sector's independence.

Tax incentives are anathema to the bureaucracy because they are not very bureaucratic. Decision-making is decentralized. The deductibility of contributions makes it possible for me to give a few more dollars than I otherwise would, but the bureaucrat does not get to tell me which college or charity to give it to. To him, my decisions seem unreliable. To me, his decisions are more apt to be crude, uneven, and uneconomic.

The movement has been in the wrong direction, toward limiting tax exemptions rather than expanding them, but a change seems to be on the way. This year we have a little more freedom on how we spend up to 30 per cent of income, if we like, on independent action. In the last session of Congress, a bill very nearly passed the Senate which would have provided a tax-credit to parents for tuition costs.

I do not see any reason why there should be any ceiling on the deductibility of contributions to independent agencies. Only the superstition that money is spent more responsibly through a central headquarters supports the deduction ceiling.

The future holds promise. Elected officials have begun to examine their right relationship to the emerging independent sector. Governor Romney is only one example. In talking about it to major figures in both parties, I have found an eager receptivity.

Their warm response may lead to a time when partisan competition will find a new dimension. Now, politicians succeed by persuading people they will use government to improve American life. But as independent action gains momentum, that emphasis may shift. Candidates may succeed by persuading people they will inspire and foster independent action. Such a candidate would design his legislative program not to constrict citizen energy but to release it.

The Republicans are, of course, more likely to adopt this new approach. They are in pain and in search of new medicine. Richard Nixon is rapidly becoming one of the independent sector's chief spokesmen. And Republicans are not inhibited, as their Democratic competitors are, by a noisy reactionary wing that still believes good things only come from government.

But the Democrats are also ready to move, as our student loan experience suggests, in the same direction. The 1964 campaign contained a fascinating paradox. The GOP made big versus limited government the central issue, and lost by a landslide. However, almost every time the Republicans offered specific proposals to get results by diffusion of responsibility from Washington, President Lyndon Johnson either chimed in or announced that he had got there first. Examples: further tax cuts, termination of the draft, the concept of bloc grants to the states.

A kind of me-tooism has begun to emerge, in the reverse direction from the past few decades. Its progress depends upon the capacity of the independent sector to form new groups for specific jobs, reach out for new responsibility, and get on with the serious business of public service.

18

Big Brotherhood
or a Free Society

It has become the fashion to wind up books about public policy by talking about the "impact of technology." Like most clichés, this one arises from an inescapable fact. We do live uneasily in what *Fortune* editor Max Ways has termed "The Era of Radical Change," and men's technology powers the change.

It is, of course, tempting to exaggerate the consequences of change. It makes good copy. Writers have made hair-raising predictions about the effects of automation, glibly forecasting that men, displaced by machines, will soon stand idle and obsolete in their own world.

Even more frightening are the predictions that technology will be used to control and homogenize men. Socialist George Orwell's vivid *1984* described a world without freedom, a world in which machines are used as instruments of tyranny to perceive and punish even the most timid expression of individuality. Orwell's book was an honest account of the consequences of the new technology if used by the political system that he described. On the conservative side, Professor Friedrich A. Hayek has pointed out that absolute tyranny has become daily more feasible. Medieval tyrants could exercise sporadic cruelty over their subjects. But sustained, total surveillance by Big Brother, with electronic eyes and brains, became possible only in recent years. Now it can be done. We will build Aldous Huxley's *Brave New World* if we do not build a free world.

Hayek and Orwell both show us that technology magnifies the threat of tyranny, or, in other words, the coming of a one-sector society. And in the United States, we are almost halfway there. A two-sector society is unstable. Saul Alinsky wanted me to title this book . . . 3-2-*1*, like a countdown. He meant that if a three-sector society becomes a two-sector society, it will then soon become a one-sector society.

We can see the symptoms. We watch liberals and conservatives thrown into acrid but arid conflict. Their valid ambitions clash and destroy each other. Political activity merely strengthens government. Conservatives are doomed to ineffectiveness, liberals driven to expand government or abandon their idealism. And the commercial sector, unprotected, stands naked in a conflict it cannot win.

As the knowledge explosion hastens change, it can only accelerate this grim process. The warfare merely moves to a higher technological level; the Orwellian nightmare becomes a preview of tomorrow.

But the coin has another side. If men carefully and deliberately use new knowledge in the independent sector, they can magnify its effectiveness many times over. The information explosion can be its salvation.

Only our central superstition pushes us in the opposite direction. It is the dogma that only government can make the powerful new technology serve the public. Science will consign us to the Orwellian hell only if government becomes the sole manager of change. Yet the superstition that only government can focus today's technology on social problems has become a mental reflex.

Recently, in the wake of cutbacks in defense contracts

for research and development in weapons and the possibility of more cuts to come, there has been speculation about how this excess talent should be put to work. One possibility widely discussed is that this fabulous know-how be applied to public problems—education, mass transportation, air-pollution control, desalting sea water, and reducing urban crime. Arthur Barber, Deputy Assistant Secretary of Defense for arms control, said: "The nation has created in the defense complexes the greatest problem-solving talent of all time. On the other hand, we have enormous problems in many areas of civilian life. It would be tragic not to bring the two together." But who will do it? Many think only government can. The president of one huge weapons corporation says: "Only governments need the large and complex systems we are organized to produce."

If this is true, the conflict which now divides us can only intensify. Liberals, in their eagerness to solve public problems, will insist that government massively apply technology to their solution. Conservatives, seeing in computerized government a multiplied threat to freedom, will intensify their Kamikaze attacks on big government. In such a continuation of the liberal-conservative impasse, men would become the helpless victims of marching robots. Technology would be the means men use to enslave each other, "to fight their way into prison," as English essayist Charles Morgan once put it.

But if, on the other hand, we put our new technology to work in a strong drive to rehabilitate the citizen's capacity for public service, the machine will be the emancipator. We can put man's new understanding to work more promptly and effectively than government can. The recent signs of a revitalized capacity for direct action suggests that technological tyranny may not be the wave of the future. Men want to use the machines, rather than be used by them.

The critical question is not, Who can use the technology? but, Who will?

We can build whatever kind of world we want. We can build the good society—prosperous, humane, free—on a scale that defies our present capacity to see the future. Step by step, as the whole society discovers new ways to use its new tools, we can turn them to purposes not yet clear to us. We know that the free economy will provide more and more of whatever people want to buy. We know that we will have more and more free time and more ways to enjoy it. Almost everybody will be able to deepen his life through artistic and creative effort. But the ultimate mark of dignity will be the use of more time, and more resources, on voluntary service. We can, indeed we must, grow as responsible individuals and regain a full sense of human purpose.

The key to these ambitions, I believe, is the independent sector.

Through it, we can restore the supportive circle whereby America originally put its unique emphasis on personal dignity. We can again insure our freedom by limiting the powers of central government. Being free, we can move to ever higher planes of prosperity and ever greater human aspirations. We can, as we learn how, focus our growing prosperity directly and imaginatively on real human needs.

We can reclaim the American dream.

Afterword

Reclaiming the American Dream was published in 1965. As I read it now, more than twenty years later, I find it gratifying and disappointing in about equal measure. It was my first book, and at the time I thought it would be my last. I was not then a writer and certainly not a scholar, but an activist of a particular kind, and what is reprinted here is clearly less a book than a case-bound, book-length tract. I do not wish in any way to apologize for it, but I am grateful for the opportunity to explain, in the more candid way my present state of mind permits, the particular circumstances of the book's genesis. Some people believe it was an influential book, and while I would like to think it was, I feel much more strongly that its central idea has not yet received nearly the attention it deserves, and in that sense *Reclaiming the American Dream* was either an anachronism or a failure or both. Needless to say, the American dream as you will find it here defined has not yet been reclaimed, but time has powerfully affirmed some of the book's propositions while it discredited others.

I will discuss what I believe are the strengths and weaknesses of the book a little further on, but first I want to explain certain ambiguities in the personal summary that serves as an introduction. The statement was included as an afterthought to squeeze the book's thesis into the context of the then current debate in a way it did not entirely deserve, and also to give the book a false confessional air, as if a dangerous reactionary had suddenly seen the error of his ways and tearfully accepted the then fashionable agenda of what we were just then beginning to call the Liberal Establishment. I admitted I had been a right-wing extremist who had swallowed the conservative doctrine whole. I hadn't been and didn't, but because the public had not even begun to distinguish between the gathering conservative movement and the then practically invisible libertarian movement of which I was a proud and industrious functionary, it seemed reasonable to borrow the conservative designation. This was a mistake, but it was not as reprehensible as it sounds now: the vague and mistaken public image of a libertarian, if one existed at all, was of a cloaked and bearded figure with a bomb behind his back and a dirty book in his pocket. Moreover, there was another compelling practical reason for the deception over which I had less control.

From the time I set aside the unexamined statist attitudes I had absorbed as a Southern California teenager, I was a libertarian, and while it is exasperating to think that a point of view that has taken half a century of thought and experience and heartbreak to work out can be summed up in a single word, I still am. It happened pretty much as it is described in the first few pages of this book. As a young man, I was laid up for a year by an illness, and I began to read more widely than I ever had before, guided by the suggestions of my older brother. As soon as I had finished college, I hurried to New York to study with Ludwig von Mises, the Austrian scholar who has lately and posthumously received some of the recognition he deserved for explaining with astonishing clarity, seventy years before the fact, the inevitability of the recent

collapse of the Soviet economy. At the time, the social-
ists had sent the celebrated Polish economist Oskar
Lange into the lists against him, and while Mises
clearly won that encounter on points, such was the
emotional appeal of socialism's promise to set right the
alleged iniquities of a capitalist order that Lange was
lionized and Mises became something of a pariah.

When I joined Mises' seminar in 1949 it was a dark
hour for libertarians and for Mises, their unanimously
acknowledged intellectual godfather. In those days,
libertarian ideas were considered not just unfashion-
able but pernicious. Mises' place in the public con-
sciousness, if he had one at all, was in leftist de-
monology. He was teaching part time at the Graduate
School of Business Administration at New York University because it was the only job he could get, and
then only when an obscure California foundation, re-
alizing that libertarian scholars were becoming ex-
tinct, had arranged to pay his stipend. Mises could afford just one subscription to the opera and he and his
wife attended alternate performances. When Mises'
monumental *Human Action* was published in 1949, the
year I joined his seminar, the *New York Times Book
Review* reproached the Yale University Press for pub-
lishing it. When Robert Heilbroner graciously acknowledged Mises' remarkable foresight in *The New
Yorker* in 1990, it was almost certainly the first time
his name had been mentioned in that discriminating
periodical. The recent collapse of the socialist
economies is in part a tribute to the tremendous power
of an intellectual movement that, forty years before,
would have fitted into a phone booth.

This is not the place to attempt a detailed description of the libertarian faith as I found it (and for me at
least it was a faith long before it became a properly ex-
amined point of view) but we believed above all that
man's power over man should be strictly limited, and

that any design for social improvement that depended on government for its execution was ill-advised to say the very least. We believed that a society had to be free before it could begin to think about being anything else, and that while logically and historically government was not freedom's only enemy, it was certainly its most experienced and effective one. We believed that a society could be safe and workable without much government, but this was a distinctly secondary concern. We were much more adept and enthusiastic at renouncing the perils and perversions of government than at explaining exactly how a society might work with less of it. We were evangelists with an intricate vision of hell, but quite an incomplete one of heaven.

We had the good or bad fortune to have found this faith at a time when practically everyone else was inclined to believe its opposite that there was very little a modern society could not accomplish if it would set aside its outmoded scruples and give the government more power, more money and more enlightened and detailed instructions. But we were very few and very young and we found this nearly unanimous opposition exhilarating.

The members of the tiny libertarian cadre of which I was a part were eager, earnest, cocksure and, I believe, absolutely harmless. We talked incessantly and never seemed to need any sleep. In spite of the fact that we were utterly powerless, we had what would now be called power lunches at which we worked out intricate strategies for altering the course of history as confidently and matter-of-factly as we might have planned a picnic or a ping-pong tournament.

At about this time (I was then in my mid twenties), I went to the West Coast to work for the remarkable middle-sized philanthropic foundation, mentioned above, that had begun to specialize in the preservation of libertarian scholarship. I had come to share completely the foundation's conviction that no social movement, or counter-movement, could go anywhere if it was not built on a solid intellectual foundation—something we had learned from Hayek whose article, "The Intellectuals and Socialism," had become a kind of field manual of libertarian tactics. So we set about finding and assisting the libertarian survivors of the inundation of Western academia, first by Marxist and then by Keynesian thought, whose adherents we found to be about as tolerant of intelligent opposition as today's multiculturalists.

For the first few years, the foundation's income comfortably exceeded our ability to find libertarian scholars and devise ways to extend their influence, but in time we looked more and more hungrily at the part of the foundation's money that had traditionally been spent to support conventional health, welfare, and educational organizations, most of them in the founder's home town in the Midwest. We began to examine these groups critically, and to plot the elimination of our support to them.

Meanwhile, I continued to repress an abiding feeling of unease that there was a screw loose somewhere in the libertarian rationale. In our incessant all-night sessions devoted to perfecting and polishing the position, again and again we were constrained to make uncomfortable choices between liberty and humanity. Our only fully developed analytical tool was market theory, and we stretched it unreasonably as we tried to make it fit every case. But sometimes, as when a hypothetical orphan was crippled by a hit and run driver, or an imaginary geriatric coal miner with no other skill lost his job when the mine closed down, market theory simply wasn't enough. And we had to decide whether to accept some sort of government program to help—or remain steadfast in our libertarian principles and do nothing. In the end I always chose liberty over community along with the other members of the movement (as with most beleaguered dissident groups, we placed a high value on the interior consistency of the libertarian canon), but privately I never felt right about it.

I say in the book that I went forth looking for some way to resolve this unsettling conflict, but actually I stumbled onto it as I looked for ways to persuade my trustees to stop wasting money on hospitals and nursing homes that was needed to propagate the faith. As I studied more closely the innumerable voluntary agencies whose requests for money filled our mailbox every day, an almost off-hand remark by an associate caused me to see suddenly that these familiar groups, however unconsciously, already constituted a kind of vestigial alternative to government action on community business. While there were (and still are) grave questions about their fitness as serious competitors for the vast responsibilities of the modern welfare state, I could begin to see in these voluntary organizations the dim outlines of a society in which those haunting, morally intolerable midnight choices between liberty and community would not have to be made.

In a few months, my idea of how I wanted to pursue the libertarian vision changed entirely. I began to see that libertarians, whether they liked it or not or even whether they understood it or not, were involved not in an argument, but in a practical competition for results. I suddenly realized that the (usually unwritten) preamble to every proposal to enlarge government's responsibilities was a rarely challenged assumption that nongovernmental means were inadequate to whatever task was under discussion—whether it was the protection of depositors from the imprudence of their bankers, the allocation of radio frequencies, shelter for the homeless, or the rehabilitation of drug addicts. Voluntary action on the public business was every day being declared unfit for serious social responsibility without a hearing. I began to understand that whereas libertarians had come to believe that good societies could be legislated (or, at least, their statist counterpart could be de-legislated), in fact they have to be built—that in the end the only practical way to make a modern state less large was to starve it of responsibility. I set forth on a mission that, in retrospect, made the endeavors of Don Quixote seem sane and feasible. I was then about thirty.

It was clear early in the game that the public was largely unaware of the voluntary sector. Any claim that it had large possibilities for constructive social action would be incredible without some practical demonstrations of what the sector could do. So I made plans to do some things the state was doing or was about to do and do them better. The first such undertaking, described in some detail in this book, was to organize a non-governmental mechanism to meet the need for low-cost educational loans to students who for one reason or another were ineligible for bank credit, thus competing head-on with a federal student loan program established by the National Defense Education Act of 1958. At the same time, we began to develop a number of other experimental programs—one to identify and place people who were then called the hard-core unemployed, another to provide good houses for very poor people at very low cost, and an ingenious scheme for nongovernmental urban renewal, among others.

By 1963, the student loan program was working well. With our guarantee, two-thirds of the nation's banks were making low-cost loans to any needy student whose college would simply stipulate was likely to finish his or her course of study. The early results from the other more ambitious experiments were encouraging. By then I had no doubt that voluntary, non-

profit organizations could in time offer serious alternatives to all the programs of the welfare state, and I
wrote *Reclaiming the American Dream*. By the fall of
1964, I had submitted the manuscript to eight publishers. Seven had rejected it and one had lost it altogether. Then Barry Goldwater was defeated in his run
for the presidency by one of history's most memorable
margins.

Goldwater's candidacy had been doomed from the
outset; it was a sort of accident that he was running at
all. Not long after John Kennedy's election, strategists
for the discontented conservative wing of the Republican Party began to study the conservative outlook for
1964. They found it surprisingly encouraging. The
South did not like Kennedy, and conservative pollsters
could prove on paper that he would have serious trouble against a conservative candidate. At a now famous
meeting in Chicago, Goldwater agreed to run, and, on
the strength of that commitment, a group of conservative organizers led by F. Clifton White began their astonishing takeover of the Republican Party.

President Kennedy's assassination and Lyndon
Johnson's ascension changed the political prospect totally. Against Johnson, Goldwater had no chance, and
he knew it from the beginning. But his supporters,
blinded by their unlikely early success, implored
Goldwater to keep his promise to them and he did.

The unpromising Goldwater candidacy aroused the
left's subliminal paranoia, and a desperate and sometimes ugly campaign was launched against him. *Look*
magazine was in the vanguard, and when Goldwater
was not just defeated but obliterated, I think the editors feared that in their zeal to destroy Goldwater they
might have destroyed two-party politics. One of *Look's*
principal writer/editors at the time was T George Harris, who has since become a celebrated launcher and
fixer of popular magazines. I had met George some

years before when he had been chief of the *Time-Life* bureau in San Francisco. He had become interested in what we were doing, followed it closely, and had from time to time proposed that *Look* publish something about the small revolution we were trying to foment. But Harris had had no encouragement until Goldwater's overwhelming defeat left *Look*'s editors looking for something to say that might help resuscitate their stricken adversary, as a victorious boxer might help his opponent off the floor. Harris quickly reshaped the material to serve this purpose and in December 1964, about a month after the election, it was published under the title, "The New Conservative Manifesto." The article was an unexpected sensation in the smallish world of people who take public affairs seriously. *Look* got more mail than any piece of that sort had ever generated before, virtually all of it enthusiastic, and I became, for a mercifully short time, a kind of bush league celebrity.

Random House promptly bought *Reclaiming the American Dream*, and I began to receive altogether unprecedented numbers of letters, telephone calls and propositions of various kinds, many of them from politicians. In this way, a movement that was not conservative came to be called conservative, and a nonpolitical, even antipolitical approach to public policy came to be seen as a new and promising political strategy. My judgment having been clouded by the unaccustomed attention, I agreed to these misrepresentations, an error I have since come to regret most deeply. The untruth in labeling was of course much less important than the unnatural politicalization of a position that will not succeed until it is understood, not just as nonpolitical, but as counterpolitical. This became the principal defect of the movement and the book.

The body of the book has eighteen short chapters which, although they are not so divided in the contents, fall into five parts. The first part consists of three chapters that describe the then emerging American dilemma. American liberalism and American conservatism were moving toward separate dead ends for the same reason: the apparent absence of any alternative to government action on a seemingly endless agenda of public problems. Thus, conservatives seemed to be indifferent to the needs of people and liberals seemed blind to the limitations and hazards of big government, and the public was losing its confidence in both.

The second part, which consists of seven chapters (4 through 10), introduces the half-forgotten voluntary alternative to government action on public problems, touches on its rise and fall in the American experience, proposes a name and a preliminary definition for this independent sector, explains its metabolism and suggests that the institutions that comprise it must become aggressive competitors for public responsibility if we are ever to define the public business sensibly and deal with it effectively.

The third part, consisting of two chapters (11 and 12), describes our impudent effort to compete head-on with the federal student loan program, and proposes a battle plan for similar efforts in other fields.

The four chapters of the fourth part (13 through 16) describe promising independent possibilities for four groups of institutions—businesses, churches, existing independent organizations and foundations. This section is naturally the most dated.

The two closing chapters (17 and 18) I find least satisfactory. The first develops an idea I now believe to be transparently mistaken—namely that chief executive officers of political jurisdictions have a natural and essential responsibility to promote independent alternatives to governmental initiatives. The final chapter hints at one essential proposition:

that the survival of the two better understood dimensions of pluralism—political democracy and free markets—may depend on our ability to redevelop pluralism's third, least familiar, form: independent action on public problems. The rest of the chapter, having to do with technology, is without merit and simply reminds me unpleasantly that I tried and failed to find a satisfactory way to end the book.

The book's point of departure—that America's liberals and conservatives had both become irrelevant to the course of the nation's affairs for the same reason—is now more valid than in 1965, when Irving Kristol had only recently been mugged by reality and deserted the liberal ranks. The worried ambivalence a few of us were beginning to notice then has now become a widely acknowledged national crisis.

The thirties and forties and fifties produced a large, ardent literature that imagined the boundless possibilities of activist government. The sixties, when *Reclaiming the American Dream* was published, saw the beginnings of a literature of an entirely different sort—sadder, saner, sometimes hair-raising chronicles of the failures of the state's efforts to improve society. Now the literature documenting the failure of state action has become almost as immense and impenetrable as government itself.

The American welfare state, an undertaking now at least three times as large as the whole Soviet economy, is no longer sustained either by logic or any record of practical success. It is becoming clear that we have confused the state's blustering eagerness to take responsibility with an innate capacity to exercise it. The American polity, along with most of the developed world's democracies, is in a bind from which there is no apparent escape. The status quo is impossible to defend and impossible to change.

We seem closer than ever to the dead end I described almost three decades ago, and intellectuals of whatever persuasion are unequipped to deal with it. The radical left, never a significant force in America, is taking its grand design back to the drawing board. The moderate left, ever oblivious, failing still to understand the question, pauses to label the now unarguable economic incompetence of the state a paradox, and continues its familiar effort to heap ever larger burdens on government.

America's free market advocates, an uneasy coalition of conservatives and libertarians, find themselves speechless. The conservative wing has already surrendered. The Reagan administration marked the end of an era, but it was not the one most pundits meant. It did not signal the end of expanding government; only the end of an era of pretense that government spending could be controlled. The so-called Reagan revolution was counterfeit—a tax revolt in disguise. Reagan's important constituents were not the rich but the recipients of the escalating middle-class entitlements that had become the primal source of big budgets and high taxes. Reagan's mission was not to repeal the welfare state but to preserve it, and to substitute debt or inflation for taxation as a way of paying its politically irreducible costs. And the American welfare state, in spite of the fact that it is not working and that its costs are undermining the economic base that supports it, marches on without effective opposition.

After decades of believing they could reshape society by the way they voted, Americans have become disaffected not merely with particular parties or politicians, but with the political process itself. Substantial majorities no longer believe important national problems—inflation, energy shortages, crime—can be solved through political action. The collapse of confidence in what we have relied on so exclusively for so long has left a dark and dangerous void. One begins to hear again those chilling calls for strong leadership, the only apparent alternative to a paralyzed political system.

Moving to the second part, chapters 4 through 10, which introduce and explain the independent sector, I would not wish to change beyond rephrasing the contention in chapter 4 that the American dream is best defined as a society that is free, prosperous, and responsible. The more I read about nineteenth and early twentieth-century America, the more I am convinced that we were on the way to achieving this ideal when American society had three ambitious sectors, and that without an aggressive third sector, these essential ambitions are incompatible. I am more than ever certain that the revival of the independent sector is essential to the survival of American society.

The historical sketch of the independent sector in chapter 4 is very weak, but that is not entirely my fault. The historical literature on independent action, the aspect of American society so many foreign observers thought most distinctive and important, is thin and uneven. We know the sector flourished in the nineteenth century. We know that the progressive movement had two distinct branches—one statist and one voluntarist—of comparable intellectual vigor. We know that before America's Great Depression, there appears to have been a formidable alternative to government action for almost every aspect of the public business, from disease control to economic stabilization. And we know that by 1958, in *The Affluent Society*, John K. Galbraith could write about American society as if it had only two sectors—one public, by which he meant governmental, and the other private, by which he meant commercial—and that no one noticed the omission for years.

How we could lose a sector of this size and scope is something of a mystery. Perhaps the decline of this dimension of our pluralism began when Woodrow Wilson set out to use his extraordinary wartime powers to jail all our most gallant, original, and entertaining misfits and rationalize American society. By 1946, the American tradition of independent, nongovernmental action on the public business had been buried alive—an accidental casualty of Wilson, two world wars that greatly improved the health of the state, a thoroughly demoralizing depression, and, finally, the politically captivating Keynesian contention that, in a presumably mature economy, government spending was often its own justification, giving government a decisive advantage in the continuing contention for social responsibility. But the details of these phenomena are waiting to be written.

Chapter 5 introduces the term independent sector. When I started thinking about the sector, it had no name. I made a list of a number of possibilities that I carried around in my pocket, asking anybody who would listen for their views and preferences. One day, sitting in the King Cole bar in the St. Regis hotel in New York, a table or two away from Salvador Dali, I went over the list with the late Frank S. Meyer, once a Communist Party organizer at Cambridge and when I knew him still a sort of double agent—a conservative with uncommonly cordial relations with the libertarians. We decided together that while independent sector wasn't perfect, I would probably never find anything better, so I tore up the list and stopped looking.

The term seems to be working its way into the language very slowly, and still competes with other terms, most notably the third sector or the voluntary sector. Sociologist Peter Berger, regrettably, I think, refers to the institutions of the independent sector as mediating structures. A national organization that is becoming ever more visible calls itself Independent Sector, and while I find that choice gratifying in a way, it is also misleading. Let me explain what I mean.

The whole independent sector consists of a number of specialized subsectors, some of which are much more sharply defined and visible than others. By far the most visible subsector of the independent sector is that supported by donations. This charitable or philanthropic subsector consists of about three-quarters of a million formally organized agencies, necessarily highly visible because they must continuously solicit money from the public and, increasingly, from various levels of government. It is almost universally mistaken for the whole. When a governmental or independent commission to examine the independent sector is set up—in my lifetime there have been the Cox Committee and the Reece Committee, both governmentally sponsored and financed; and the Peterson Commission and most recently the Filer Commission, both independently sponsored and financed—they have invariably treated the philanthropic subsector as if it alone comprised the independent sector. But these familiar charitable agencies, which (along with their philanthropic benefactors) constitute the whole constituency of Independent Sector, represent only a specialized fraction of the sector. They are atypical in a number of important ways that I will discuss a little later.

The most difficult chapter was the sixth, called "The Independent Sector," and it would be difficult today. Jason Epstein, my editor at Random House, had told me with characteristic acumen and bluntness that I had written a book about something I had defined but not described. It has become a familiar problem, one I encounter every time I write or talk about the independent sector. I have written three books, a number of articles and over the years made scores of speeches and lectures about it, and have never learned how to describe, with reasonable brevity and force, the endlessly vast, varied and entirely unfamiliar territory I am talking or writing about. It is an inevitable consequence of the curiously limited awareness of the sector and its possibilities, and will remain unsolved until the institutions and activities of the third sector are as familiar to the public as those of the other two.

That first time I tried, I spent days in my room at the University Club in New York City, filling wastebaskets with failed efforts to describe a whole, complex, contradictory, largely forgotten world in a few breezy paragraphs suitable to a short, inspirational book. Chapter six is the unsatisfactory result. I did not know then, nor do I know now, the full extent of the independent sector, and what you will find is a partial and hence somewhat misshapen view of it. I expect public awareness of the sector will develop slowly and continuously as mine is still developing, and will never be complete.

The next few chapters 7-11, although written in the same evangelistic style as the rest of the book, are theoretical. The illustrative material is a third of a century old, but I think the propositions set forth have been affirmed by the experience of the years between. It seems ever more clearly true that without some alternative to the state actively contending for responsibility, the public business can neither be reasonably defined nor responsibly dealt with.

The radical message of *Reclaiming the American Dream* was that in the long run political democracy and free markets would not survive unless the independent sector began to compete aggressively with the state for all—or practically all—its responsibilities. I was convinced that this kind of competition *was* the elusive humanist revolution everybody was talking about. I wasn't saying we should start this revolution;

I was saying we were already in it—and losing, and moreover that much of the sector had already surrendered. Given the sector's lack of self-consciousness and its utter incapacity for collective decision making, the idea that independent institutions would rise up and wrest responsibility from Leviathan was of course a pipe dream, and there is little evidence that anyone outside our inner circle took it seriously.

Fans of the book who thought of themselves as liberals believed I had defined a resource that would be a useful supplement to the welfare state (Beatrice Webb viewed the state as a great extension ladder of which voluntary agencies comprise the last, most slender section), but rejected absolutely the idea that we should undertake to supplant it. Fans of the book who thought of themselves as conservatives found its propositions useful as political rhetoric, but were unready to act on them. Most of my libertarian friends were willing to discuss possible market solutions to public problems, but, lacking any analytical device but market theory, continued to believe that anything that could not be done profitably should probably not be done at all.

In short, although the book attracted some attention, in the end its readers found its primary contention unacceptable. But a few of us remained convinced that the independent sector could, if it would, develop superior alternatives to the activities of the welfare state. I and a handful of companions continued our lonely battle for the responsibility to guarantee loans to students whose needs were beyond the reach of the market.

In the end, United Student Aid Funds, our flagship effort to compete with government, was an illuminating failure. The organization still exists, and, as this is written, it has just finished a new headquarters building in Indianapolis to house its 1500 employees. It has guaranteed more than $3 billion in student loans, but it long ago gave up the mission we intended for it. What we built in the hope it would be an alternative to the state became, as have a great many independent organizations in our time, an instrument of the state.

Chapter 11 outlines the effort's history until 1965, when the Johnson administration's education bill, which in its first version would have overwhelmed us, was revised to embody a compromise we had proposed—namely that the federal government would provide guaranteed student loans only when the independent response was inadequate. But there was a catch: The revised version of the bill made the Department of Education, our potential competitor, the judge of the adequacy of our response. We went to work desperately to substitute an objective definition of adequacy for the subjective judgement of our adversary, and in the end we succeeded. The law specified adequate loan amounts, adequately low interest rates, adequately generous terms of repayment, even adequate proximity to a participating bank. It may have been the first time in history that adequacy was precisely defined in legislation in a nation that had professed for years that its government should act only if nongovernmental means were inadequate. (Incidentally, we found to our great consternation that it would have been illegal for United Student Aid Funds to defend its right to compete before the Congress. I was obliged to cut my official ties to the organization and establish and finance another, the Council of Private Lending Institutions, which could lobby legally, to make the case for our survival.)

That legislative battle won and the terms of the competition clearly defined, we believed briefly that our troubles were over—that we had only to work hard to stay adequate. We had no idea that our competitors, utterly convinced that the public interest would be better served by a federal monopoly, would compete unfairly and dishonorably. We found ourselves in a game of political hard ball, in which federal representatives literally conspired to create artificial surges in the demand for guarantees so that, state by state, our program could be ruled technically inadequate and the federal programs activated. Had not our lawyers had the foresight to include a provision that obliged these bogus federal initiatives to be withdrawn when independent resources became adequate under the law, we would have been more promptly displaced.

What overwhelmed us eventually was something we had not expected and were helpless to fight against. What had been a more or less responsible contention for a legitimate community responsibility was moved to the great brawling arena of pork-barrel politics: the federal government moved to extend eligibility for guaranteed loans from a large but manageable number of authentically needy students to the whole, broad American middle class where the votes are. In time, as we predicted repeatedly before congressional committees, the federal guarantee program became a monstrosity.

The extension of guarantees to commercially qualified borrowers took the game into territory where we could not compete and did not wish to compete. What was undoubtedly good politics was highly irresponsible public policy as the dimensions of the student loan scandal now make clear. Our bold scheme to beat the government at its own game was in the end an instructive failure. It helped me understand that several decades of well-intentioned effort to produce a responsible society through activist government had in the end produced something grotesque—an unworkable, unaffordable and untouchable welfare state—and that the substitution of independent for government action would be rather more difficult than I had imagined.

When the roots of our present welfare state were planted in the thirties, the underlying policy premise was that the beneficiaries were poor and the benefactors rich. But since World War II, that supposition has disguised a great metamorphosis, as the beneficiaries and the benefactors have become more and more the same people. Now, increasingly, the poor, whose plight continues to provide the rationalization for the myriad programs of the welfare state, are rarely its principal beneficiaries and the rich, whose conspicuous consumption suggests a boundless ability to pay, are no longer its principal benefactors.

America's political demographics have evolved into something disturbing. There is an underclass, small and inert enough to be inconsiderable politically, whose problems seem increasingly chronic, intractable, and uninteresting. There is a sprawling, politically invincible middle class, the members of which are increasingly unwilling to pay for a wide range of state-provided services to which they believe they are entitled and which moreover could probably be provided by the free market, if one existed, for much less money. And there is a small but highly visible upper class grudgingly sheltered from the full force of taxation because their continued investments in the economy seem to be an important source of what remains of its vitality. The rise of this mass middle-class welfare state has made undertakings like ours at the same time much more important and much more difficult.

The federal establishment is a vast impenetrable thicket of literally thousands of separate programs—from tea tasting to Medicare. Lacking some sure and objective way of defining the public business and allocating responsibility to whichever institutions are best able to take it, this forest of federal programs will continue to be a hopeless tangle of undertakings the market could probably do better, tasks the independent sector could do better, things that do not need to be done at all, and a residue of tasks only the government can do. We are sinking under the weight of a federal establishment we cannot afford economically and cannot alter politically. The government's responsibilities have outgrown its resources and thus economic crisis, in one form or another, has become endemic.

In our failed student loan initiative, we may have left a small legacy of experience on how, in another, saner time, the public business might be defined and assigned more sensibly.

Our operation had clearly established its relationship to the government sector by its detailed definition of adequacy. The government's responsibility became one of auditing our adequacy, a function it could be relied on to perform enthusiastically whether it was specified in the law or not. We could maintain our franchise only by meeting that standard. But we had identified a borderline on our other side as well—our territorial relationship to the commercial sector. It was in a way a more natural one. Our borrowers got their money from their hometown banks, which our guarantee enabled to lend (at an interest rate calculated cover the banks' costs) to students whose families did not qualify for commercial loans. If a student whose family did qualify brought one of our guarantee applications to a bank, the bank would forward it to us with a notation that it was willing to make a conventional loan and we would withhold our guarantee. Thus we didn't use philanthropic resources to support loans to students the market was willing to provide. We were helping all those, but only those who were demonstrably, case by case, beyond the reach of the market. We weren't undermining the market; we were extending its reach. We achieved—momentarily—a rational distribution of responsibility among the state, the market and the independent sector.

Chapter 12, "How to Compete With Government" was intended as a kind of field manual for anyone who might want to try, as we did, to reduce the role of the state by taking some responsibility away from it. I am not aware that anyone else did or plans to.

The next four chapters deal, in turn, with business and its relation to the independent sector, with the institutions of the philanthropic or charitable subsector, with the church and with foundations. I would not now write any of them in quite the same way. There has been a steady increase in business involvement in the affairs of the independent sector, either directly or as benefactors of its more visible institutions, but to little effect. In time, the entrepreneurs among us may realize that the survival of the free markets in which they operate depends above all on a renaissance of independent action on a grand scale. Then we might see the kind of social reconstruction the times require—bold, believable initiatives to substitute private for public programs in health care, economic stabilization, retirement security, education and other central programs of the welfare state.

I have not much hope for the philanthropic or charitable subsector. These groups on the whole have, in my admittedly radical view, misunderstood their mission and their right relation to the state. Regrettably, the public's attitudes toward the independent sector are shaped by the activities of this most visible cluster of organizations, but it is untypical of what the sector is now and of what it may some day become. Agencies of this subsector are sustained primarily by money contributions, while most of the larger independent sector is much less dependent on monetary support. They are

usually staffed by professionals; volunteers are most
often used as fundraisers or policymakers. The agencies of the philanthropic subsector raise money with
which they hire professionals to administer some social
or health or educational service to clients—often
primarily middle-class clients. It is only marginally
unfair to say that these charitable agencies are hard to
distinguish from government agencies and, in fact,
they are increasingly financed by government. (The
agencies under the United Way umbrella in the major
cities receive almost half their money from
government—in New York City, more than two thirds.)
Most of the agencies in the philanthropic subsector of
the independent sector have become quasi-
governmental.

This subsector has received and spent about two
percent of GNP for many years. Because it is cash intensive, its rate of growth has necessarily been slow. It
is widely perceived as threatened or endangered,
something to be rescued from extinction like the
whooping crane or preserved, like a decaying cathe-
dral. E.M. Forster once mocked the Quakers for op-
posing Armageddon with philanthropy, and any sug-
gestion that these endangered entities might somehow
remedy the great systemic failures of the welfare state
seems equally absurd.

The present leaders of the philanthropic subsector
would hasten to agree. Waldemar Nielsen stated the
matter with jarring clarity in his book *The Endangered
Sector:*

> The old era of *laissez-faire* pluralism is therefore beyond
> doubt past. The new era is one of socialization and
> politicalization, of complexity and interconnection. A time
> of planned, governmentalized, officially subsidized and
> guided pluralism is upon us. Nonprofit institutions, as one
> element in a society in radical transition, will never again

be the same in status, relative scale, function, or
autonomy.
Most of the Third Sector—including all of its great in-
stitutionalized elements except the churches—must
henceforth live within the embrace of, and to a significant
degree as dependents and instruments of, government.
That situation already and unmistakably obtains, and
there is no plausible basis for supposing that it can be
reversed—or indeed that either party to the relationship
wishes to reverse it. The leaders of most of the major
categories of the Third Sector institutions want more
government money, not less, and are fully prepared to
accept the regulatory consequences.

I believe this view, in my experience nearly universal among those prominent in the philanthropic subsector, is short-sighted, self-defeating, and almost totally mistaken. The sector must see itself not as an instrument of the state but as an essential alternative to
the state. The leaders of the charitable subsector hold
out a vision of a comfortable future in the arms of the
state, but pluralism becomes pretense when one sector
of a professed pluralistic polity becomes dependent on
another. A chastened, captive, and obedient pluralism
is worse that no pluralism at all. The leaders of
Poland's Solidarity took a final stand on this issue.
They insisted that the state was not the society. When
Westerners urged Solidarity's leaders to collaborate
with the state to avoid bloody confrontation, Solidarity's Zbigniew Bujah told *The New York Times* in a
smuggled interview that collaboration would have
made Solidarity another annex of the totalitarian system, creating only an impression of democracy.

The independent sector must come to see itself as
elementally different from the state, with a prior, more
powerful moral franchise than the state. Its means
seem more fragile than the state's irresistible powers
to tax and command, but they are in the long run more
legitimate and powerful. The sector cannot fulfill its
essential mission until it detaches itself from the state.

Perhaps there needs to be a rigid, even constitutionally defined and protected doctrine of separation of the independent sector and the state.

The sector as a whole has no self-consciousness—or nearly none—no accurate sense of its own size and scope, and no sense of its right relationship to other institutions. It has no leaders, no secretariat, and no voice. So when representatives for the charitable subsector—the most captive, arthritic, and unadventurous—speak, they seem to speak for the whole. They seem much more concerned that the public understand the sector's limitations than its extraordinary possibilities.

Chapter 15 deals with churches. If I were writing it now, I would put much greater emphasis on the importance of churches' strict, constitutionally defined two-way separation from the state. They are, for this reason, the only segment of the independent sector whose independence is more or less intact. The churches take no money from the state and are constitutionally free of interference by the state. It is no accident that it is the churches that are offering the most extensive alternatives to public education, the largest and most impenetrable state monopoly, and the most vigorously defended state prerogative.

The data and the illustrative material in Chapter 16, about foundations, is stale and dated, but I would not alter the chapter's central contention. Most foundations still use their unusual independence to promote the expansion of the state, at a time when all the more exciting and promising opportunities are in the opposite direction.

Chapter 17, which suggests political leaders have a primary role in promoting voluntary action, I now believe to be entirely wrong, and I can scarcely believe I didn't recognize it at the time. I was influenced in part by my first-hand knowledge that president Franklin

Roosevelt had been the moving force in the independent sector's conquest of poliomyelitis, and my discovery that Herbert Hoover had repeatedly used his presidential influence to promote nongovernmental initiatives. But I'm afraid I was most affected simply by the intense and immediate interest politicians and their handlers showed in *Reclaiming the American Dream.*

The chapter describes my encounter with George Romney. A year later, in 1966, Ronald Reagan called me soon after he won the Republican nomination for governor of California, and some of the book's propositions found their way into Reagan's campaign speeches. At about that time I put together a little paperback called *If I Am Elected, I Will...* suggesting a number of specific ways the political sector might promote the independent sector.

Robert Finch, an acquaintance of mine from college, ran successfully for Lieutenant Governor in California at the same time, and he became for a time the most enthusiastic political advocate of the independent sector. In 1968, he and I hastily put together a not very good book called *The New Liberal/Conservative Manifesto,* in which we tried to define more precisely the politicians' responsibility to the independent sector. Finch had for years been Richard Nixon's principal advisor and ran his 1972 campaign. The need for a greater voluntary response to the nation's social agenda was a major campaign theme. Immediately after Nixon's victory, in the manner president Kennedy had pioneered, a number of transitional task forces were set up to make policy recommendations for the new administration in the usual fields. Arthur Burns, who headed the operation, asked me to organize an unusual task force on voluntary action and I did. I took pains to invite some Democrats to give the undertaking a less partisan cast. The group included Irving

Kristol, Max Ways of *Fortune* magazine, Richard Goodwin and about a dozen others. Burns seemed particularly interested in what we were doing and, I understand uniquely among the task forces, all our recommendations were accepted and acted upon.

Soon there was a standing Cabinet Committee on Voluntary Action, a White House Office on Voluntary Action, which we had taken pains to explain should have a diplomatic, rather than directive relationship to the sector. This office was to keep the president informed as to the capacities of the independent sector, report on the impact of federal programs, existing and proposed, on the independent sector, and from time to time propose ways the president could use his influence in the service of the independent sector. Romney, then secretary of housing and urban development, who was to oversee these new initiatives, was also authorized to form and finance privately an umbrella group outside government, called I believe the Voluntary Action Center. We had imagined that this would eventually become a coalition of the whole independent sector, which could enlarge public awareness of the sector and its possibilities and in time perhaps mount ambitious joint initiatives. I was sure we had at last succeeded in building a platform from which a great renaissance of independent action could be launched.

But that was a naive and idle expectation. The elaborate machinery we prematurely put in place has been scrapped. There is an enduring illusion of political interest in the independent sector because politicians instinctively want to associate themselves with voluntary efforts, but have neither the means nor the inclination to expand its scope. I cannot imagine why I thought for a moment that the state could be persuaded to contrive its own undoing. Republican presidential candidates since Nixon have continued to talk about voluntary action, but their glib and misleading characterizations—"a thousand points of light" is the most recent—have proved in practice to be only a way politicians can identify themselves with activities to which many Americans still feel a nostalgic attachment. But there have been no significant practical results.

It all reached a kind of comic apogee with Ronald Reagan's half-informed exhortation in the first year of his administration that private initiatives pick up some of the slack as the rate of growth of the welfare state slowed somewhat. White House aides were said to be optimistic that charitable giving will increase to fill the gap left by the budget cuts. But an even wider gap divided that expectation and the judgment of the leaders of the charitable agencies themselves. Representatives of the philanthropic subsector began to tell anyone who would listen that this was not a realistic expectation but a laughable one.

C. William Verity, the chairman of the committee Reagan had appointed to find alternatives to federal programs (who had earlier said he understood his role to be "sort of stirring the pigeons") told the press, It is unrealistic to expect us to fill what is not just a gap but a chasm. *The New York Times* reported: "Leaders of private charities say they will not be able to meet President Reagan's challenge to raise enough money for the needy and provide enough volunteers to offset cuts in federal social programs." Brian O'Connell, president of Independent Sector, said on cue, "It would be a disservice to the president and the public to exaggerate what voluntary organizations can do." When the dust had settled it appeared that when the president had called on the independent sector to help roll back the welfare state, it responded that it could not and would not, and moreover begged him to stop threatening to reduce the rate of increase of the federal grants on which it had come to rely.

In the personal summary, I mention how, at twenty-seven, I could not accept the pessimism of an older man, then seventy-five, for whom I had tremendous admiration and who believed the American dream was a lost cause. I'm now sixty-five, uncomfortably aware that most of my life is behind me, and I find I still can't share his bleak estimate of the American prospect. I'm troubled by what America is, but still hopeful about what it may become.

While I think we may be somewhat closer to reclaiming the American dream than we were when I wrote the book, it will be a much, much longer and more complex process than I then imagined. I think it was far too soon then and still too soon now for the sort of social transfiguration I recklessly tried to bring about in the fifties. I think the sector's practical possibilities will continue to be quite limited until some impractical preliminaries are attended to. We need to reconstruct the sector's lost history. And above all we need an intellectual revolution before its practical counterpart will have a chance. While there can no longer be any doubt about the existence of a third sector (as there were when I wrote this book), there are everywhere understandable doubts about its possibilities. Given the present state of social thought, it is as hard to believe in the utility and virility of independent social action as it was to believe in the rationality and moral legitimacy of free markets before *The Fable of the Bees* and *The Wealth of Nations*. We need now to understand voluntary social process as completely as we understand market process.

But the principal obstacle to a revival of independent action is simply its ruined condition. In a kind of institutional variation of Gresham's law, ineffective government programs tend to drive out effective independent ones. So, after half a century of headlong transfers of social responsibility to the state, the sector is in great disrepair. Its abiding dilemma is that it will not win public confidence until its competence is more clear and believable—and it cannot begin to rehabilitate itself without public confidence.

Richard Cornuelle

CPSIA information can be obtained at www.ICGtesting.com

264107BV00005B/8/P